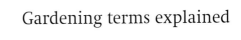

Gardening terms explained

For Mamgu and Mum

Gardening terms explained

BY JOANNA THOMAS

WESTON PUBLISHING

Gardening terms explained

First edition 2001

ISBN 0 - 9530130 - 3 - 0

Copyright © Joanna Thomas, Weston Publishing Limited

Designed and illustrated by John Miles

Printed and bound in the UK
by Butler & Tanner, Frome and London

Foreword

Gardening is not an exact science (or art, for that matter) but the uninitiated often think it is. Perhaps we gardeners are at fault for not explaining ourselves; if this is true then this book remedies the fault.

Here you can learn anything from what is the difference between silt and clay, how to identify a cordate leaf or define a monocarpic plant, why you should worry about rhizomorphs and how to take special care of your crumb structure.

Admirably bridging the notorious gap between the botanist and the gardener (why are so few of one also the other?), Jo Thomas has produced a really useful work of reference destined to be well-thumbed. Add to this the delightful pencil drawings and I am happy to recommend this unique book to any gardener. May every member of my staff write as well.

SUE MINTER

Curator, Chelsea Physic Garden

Contents

Author's note

When I first got into gardening, I didn't have a clue what I was doing. I was anxious to sow my seeds or feed my plants in the 'correct' way, mainly to ensure the survival of my newly acquired plants/gems and because, for my sins, I am a bit of a perfectionist at heart!

I read magazines and books on creating a riotous/colourful window box display or growing my own tasty herbs from seeds, but I kept coming across words and phrases that I didn't understand. I also felt a little stupid asking countless questions at the local garden centre, so I pored over gardening books to seek explanations. How could I not know the difference between top dressing and base dressing? People have been gardening quite easily for centuries!

So, I wanted to provide *one* book with all the gardening expressions explained clearly and concisely for all those budding enthusiasts out there.

After all, less time spent researching means more time spent in the garden creating our little bit of paradise!

So what have I created? A book divided into chapters and sections which cover a wide range of horticultural subjects. A few terms have been included in more than one section if necessary and this is shown clearly in the index. As far as possible in a 'pocket-size' book, I have defined and explained each term, but for more information or explanation please refer to the 'further reading' list.

The hardest, and the easiest, part of writing this book has been what to leave out. There are no names of plants as this is outside the scope of this book. I have generally not included trade names of fertilisers or pesticides because there are so many, with new ones being introduced or old ones taken off the market almost monthly. As for pests and diseases, I have only included common names, not Latin names, as these are the most commonly used. This book is by no means exhaustive, but does include the most extensively used terms on an amateur and basic professional level.

Please note that gardening terms are open to interpretation and can change over the years. This may be down to different dialects, geographical areas, gardening practices or training methods. Gardening should also be open to interpretation and change, so please take this book as providing the basics for understanding gardening, and then go out and experiment.

Acknowledgements

The author gives many thanks to the following:

Christopher Leach, my technical editor. Thank you for being so thorough, informative and understanding, you are a gentleman of the highest order. Terry Weston, you have been the instigator and driver of this project at every stage. Thank you. John Miles, the book's designer. Although we didn't have any face to face contact, a lot of your comments came back to me, they were real morale boosters. Thank you for creating such imaginative illustrations. Simon Vyle, my technical editor for fruit, pests and diseases. You are a fantastic teacher with an unaccountable wealth of knowledge. You were teaching this stuff when I was still in short pants! I will sorely miss you.

Simon Rennie, who gave me my first gardening job, Mary Thorp and all my colleagues at RBG Kew, and the Capel Manor staff and tutors who taught me so much.

Fiona Crumley for being so understanding, and everyone at the Chelsea Physic Garden for their enthusiasm and help.

Mum for giving me her genes of pedantry and Max for his nurture on how to be logical and organised.

Dougy, what can I say, thanks for not listening to my rantings, ignoring me chewing my fingers to shreds and for the cups of coffee and trips to Sainsburys. And for those intense Science lessons. I love you.

To Walch, Soph, Fabes, Erwin, Johanna, Sares, Clara, Stephen, Manda, Vicki, Lucy, Netty and Kirsty, all of your comments and support kept me going and inspired me, thank you for being my friends. I can come out now!

Finally, a dedication to all the gardeners over the decades whose knowledge I have gleaned from a myriad of books.

The publisher thanks the following for their contributions to this book.

Jo for writing the book, John Miles for the book design, illustrations and jacket design, Sue Minter for writing the Foreword and Trevor Howe for the photograph of the author.

Further thanks are due to the following for their advice and/or support, Fiona Watson, Rob Cassy and Valerie Scriven at Garden Books, Della Alim, Sofie Sutherland, Colleen Farr, Ruth Harris, Peter Towse, Louise Miles, Adrienne Maguire and Nicky Grimbly at agm marketing, Doug Badenoch at Butler and Tanner, and Kirstie Kemp and Bill Norris at Central Books.

Introduction

Introduction

Aboriculture The cultivation of trees. The term is also applied to the study of trees and tree surgery, and comes from the Latin word 'arbor' meaning 'tree'.

Angiosperm A type of plant which has evolved highly specialised methods of reproduction through seeds. These plants produce flowers and the seeds are contained within the fruit. They are the largest group of plants on earth with over two hundred and thirty thousand species.

Binomial system The system for naming plants initiated by Carl Linnaeus in the eighteenth century. He grouped plants together into families which he then divided into smaller groups called genera. He named plants using two Latin names. The first name is the genus and is given a capital letter and the second is the species name and starts with a small letter. The genus is like our surname and the species is like our first name.

Botany The study of plants including their classification, genetics, structure, ecology, distribution and economic uses.

Chimaera A plant constituted of tissues of differing genetic composition, normally two different species. It is a result of mutation or is obtained by graft hybridisation.

Classification Man's organisation of the plant kingdom into groups starting with Divisions, which are then subdivided into Classes, then Orders, Families, Genera and Species. The characteristics of plants, such as reproduction methods and flower structure, determine their classification so that they may be identified at all times. The study of plant genetics and DNA structure is now being used for plant classification (see appendix).

Common name A name given to a plant which is commonly known to a group of people within a region or country but seldom known throughout the world by the same common name. The name, which is in the country's language rather than Latin, usually has historical, cultural, social or medicinal connotations.

Cultivar A cultivated variety of a species. Most plants are adequately described by their botanical names (genus and species) but many variants still exist which differ from the species in small but distinct ways. They may have mutated spontaneously in the garden but are now mainly produced in cultivation by selection and breeding. In literature, the cultivar name follows the species name, and either has a capital letter and is shown in single quotes or is preceded by the abbreviation cv.

Dicotyledon A subclass of angiosperm which produces two seed leaves at germination and the leaf veins are usually branched.

F^1 The first generation of hybrids whereby the offspring are identical.

Family A basic division of plants grouped according to the similar structure of their flowers. Families contain sub-divisions of genera, which have distinct characteristics from each other. In literature, the family name always has a capital letter and ends in -ceae or -ae (see appendix).

Garden origin Applies to a plant that has been bred or selected and does not occur in the wild.

Gardening The craft of cultivating plants and gardens, usually as a recreational pastime.

Genus (*singular*) **genera** (*plural*) A sub-division of family grouped according to many similar plant characteristics. Genera contain sub-divisions of several or just one species. In literature, the genus name always has a capital letter (see appendix).

Graft hybrid A new hybrid plant obtained by grafting two different species. The tissues of both species mix and grow together at the point of grafting. In literature, the name of a graft hybrid is preceded by +. The term is used interchangeably with chimaera.

Group A group of named cultivars with similar characteristics. The term can also be applied to a number of similar species within a genus. The group is given a name.

Gymnosperm A type of plant which has evolved highly specialised methods of reproduction through seeds. They do not produce flowers but the seeds are contained on the outside of cones. The largest group of gymnosperms is conifers.

Horticulture The art and science of cultivating plants and gardens, usually on a professional level. The term is also applied to the study of gardening.

Hybrid A new plant obtained by the cross-fertilisation of two different species or genera. The hybrid possesses a mix of genetic material from both parents. It possesses vigour and becomes stronger than the parents and, for example, may have larger or more colourful flowers.

Intergeneric hybrid A new plant obtained by the cross-fertilisation of two different genera within the same family. The genus and species names of the plant are preceded by X.

Interspecific hybrid A new plant obtained by the cross-fertilisation of two different species within the same genera. In literature, the name of the plant contains X between the genera and species names or is given a cultivar name.

Monocotyledon A subclass of angiosperm which produces one seed leaf at germination and has parallel leaf veins.

Nomenclature The part of classification which involves the naming of orders, families, genera and species.

Permaculture A self-sustainable agricultural system developed to work with the local ecology.

Plantsman An expert in garden plants and gardening. Applies to men and women!

Series A group of plants (usually annuals) which are linked by similar features but are not identical.

Species A sub-division of genus where all the plants share distinct different characteristics. In literature, the species name has a small letter and usually describes the physical or geographical difference (see appendix).

Sub-species   A sub-division of a species where all the plants share small but distinctive differences from the type species. In literature, the sub-species name is preceded by the abbreviation ssp. (see appendix).

Variety   A variant from the species produced naturally in the wild. Most plants are adequately described by their botanical names (genus and species) but many variants still exist which differ from the species in small but distinct ways. In literature, the variety name is either shown in italics or preceded by the abbreviation var.

The environment

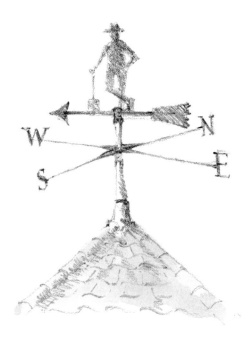

Climate and habitat

Alpine   Refers to the habitat from which a plant originates, which is any area above the tree-line on mountains in temperate, sub-tropical and tropical regions.

Arid   Refers to the habitat from which a plant originates, which loosely applies to hot desert-like areas with a long dry season.

Climate   The average weather for a region or specific locality with the seasonal differences including hours of sunshine, temperature, rainfall and humidity.

Cool-temperate   A temperate area with warm summers and cold winters.

Desiccate   When the wind takes moisture from the soil and plants and dries them out.

Drought   Lack of rainfall in a locality for an extended period.

Eddy   The flow of wind in a circular motion due to an obstruction, for example, an eddy will occur after the wind meets a row of tall trees.

Endemic   A species which is native to one restricted area and nowhere else. It occures naturally here and is not imported or introduced.

Frost   If there is a consistent temperature below freezing ($0°C$) any moisture is left as a frozen white coating. Ground frost is most common, because cold air sinks, and is where the surface and the top layer of the soil are frozen.

Frost pocket   A specific area where frost occurs more regularly than in the surrounding areas. This is due to the fact that cold air sinks so frost will occur in valleys or small dips in the garden.

Habitat   The natural environment in which a plant lives in the wild, and one which can be recreated to a certain extent in the garden.

Humidity   The moisture content in the air. When the level is high it is said to be humid, no matter what temperature it is.

Leeward The side sheltered from the wind.

Microclimate The weather within a specific locality, varying from the surrounding local or regional climate due to a change in the environment. For example, a city may have a warmer microclimate as more heat is absorbed by buildings during the day and only released slowly at night. Coastal areas have a different microclimate to those areas inland as the large bodies of water modify temperature extremes.

Native A species that grows naturally in the wild of a specific area and has not been introduced by man or other means.

Prevailing wind The most common direction from which the wind blows on average throughout the year. In the UK the prevailing wind is south westerly.

Scorching The drying and burning effect of the sun's rays on a plant, mainly the leaves.

Sub-tropical The area in the world between the temperate and tropical zones, and the term also refers to plants which originate from there. These areas have high minimum temperatures and seasonal heavy downpours of rain.

Temperate The area in the world between the polar circles and the sub-tropical zones, and the term also refers to plants which originate from there. These areas have no temperature extremes from day to night, a relatively even distribution of rainfall throughout the year and distinct seasons are a feature.

Tropical The area in the world between the Tropics of Cancer and Capricorn, and the term also refers to plants which originate from there. These areas have very high minimum temperatures and humidity, and heavy rainfall, either throughout the year or mainly in the rainy season.

Warm-temperate A temperate area with hot summers and mild winters.

Windward The side exposed to the wind.

The garden

Aspect The direction in which the garden, or part of the garden, faces. For example, if you put your back to the house and look at your garden and you are facing south, then the aspect is 'south-facing'. If you are facing west then the aspect is 'west-facing'. The aspect determines how much sun a garden can get and is therefore important when considering types of plants and their positions.

Drainage Water soaking into and through the ground. Good drainage means that surface water soaks away quickly and bad drainage means the water may sit on the surface or only drain to a shallow level, so a plant's roots may sit in the water.

Exposed site A site which is open to the wind and weather in general, for example, on the coast or the windward side of a hill.

Gradient Slope or angle.

Hard landscaping Everything in the garden that is not the plants, lawn or soil, for example, paths, gates, walls, water feature or patio.

Indicator plant A plant which is found growing naturally on a site, especially a weed species, and therefore shows a particular characteristic of the environment. It may indicate, for example, that the soil is acidic or alkaline, fertile or infertile, or contains a high proportion of one particular nutrient.

Plan An aerial view diagram of the site. It may contain existing features and/or planned features.

Shelterbelt A planted belt of trees and shrubs which provides shelter to a garden from wind, noise or pollution.

> ### TOP TIP
>
> **Making a shelter belt**
> Use mainly native plants with a mix of evergreen and deciduous trees and shrubs of differing heights and ages.

Sheltered site A site which is closed off from the wind and weather in general, for example, in the lee of a hill or surrounded by woodland.

Site analysis The process by which a site is surveyed, observed and tested.

Soft landscaping The plants, lawn and soil in the garden, as opposed to the hard landscaping.

Survey The process of measuring up a site and all the existing features within the boundary including the gradient. Most surveys also include trees and large shrubs.

Tree preservation order (TPO) An order made by the local council to preserve the life of a particular tree. It may be due to the tree's age, rarity or value to the site or environment. The tree must not be cut down without written permission, and the council also needs to be consulted on pruning.

Water table The upper level of groundwater below which the soil is saturated with water. The water table can rise after periods of prolonged heavy rain, and if it reaches the soil surface it causes flooding. Similarly, it can fall after periods of drought.

Windbreak A structure which impedes the flow of wind, for example, trees, shrubs and fences.

The soil

Soil

Acid soil   Soil which is acidic (as opposed to neutral or alkaline) because it has a high concentration of hydrogen ions, and ranges from pH0 to pH4.5. Peat soil and coarse sandy soil are naturally acidic. Gradually, soil can be made more acidic by micro-organisms which release acids into the soil and by high levels of rainfall which is slightly acidic and leaches out calcium. Calcium can also be absorbed and removed by plants.

Aeration   The amount of oxygen in the soil between soil particles and in pockets. Good aeration reduces waterlogging, increases the useful bacterial population and allows the decomposition of organic matter. Soil aeration can be improved by digging and incorporating organic matter.

Aerobic   Requiring free oxygen, for example aerobic bacteria, or containing free oxygen, for example aerobic soils.

Algae   Primitive plants without roots, stems or leaves. They are visible as a green slime on soil surfaces. They contain chlorophyll so they can photosynthesise and they thrive in moist to wet conditions.

Alkaline soil   Soil which is alkaline (as opposed to neutral or acidic) because it has a low concentration of hydrogen ions and ranges from pH8.5 to pH14. Soils derived from chalk and limestone are naturally more alkaline because they contain calcium.

Anaerobic   Not requiring free oxygen, for example anaerobic bacteria, or not containing free oxygen, for example anaerobic soils.

Bacterium (*singular*) **bacteria** (*plural*) Single-celled, microscopic soil organisms which are essential in the breakdown of organic matter into humus and the conversion of atmospheric nitrogen into forms that plants can absorb and use. Aerobic bacteria are beneficial because they require and utilise oxygen so they fully decompose organic matter. Anaerobic bacteria, on the other hand, may be detrimental to soil fertility as they do not require or utilise oxygen so they only partially decompose organic matter. They favour waterlogged soil and can create pungent 'eggy' smells. Bacteria can be saprophytic, feeding on dead organic matter, or parasitic, feeding on living organisms, or symbiotic where a mutually beneficial relationship occurs between the bacteria and living organism.

Calcareous soil Soil derived from chalk and limestone, with a high pH and therefore alkaline. These soils tend to be thin, free-draining and open soils where organic matter is rapidly broken down.

Calcicole plant One which prefers alkaline soil.

Calcifuge plant One which dislikes alkaline soil.

Calcium (Ca) A major element and nutrient which is abundant in most soils, especially those derived from chalk or limestone, although acid soils lack sufficient calcium for most plants. Plants use soluble forms of calcium, particularly in the construction of cell walls.

Calcium carbonate A white insoluble solid chemical compound which occurs naturally as chalk or limestone. Manufactured forms are sometimes referred to as carbonate of lime. It is a source of the nutrient calcium as well as helping to reduce soil acidity or improve the crumb structure of clay soils.

Cap A hard horizontal layer of soil on the soil surface through which roots cannot grow. A cap is produced by compaction after heavy rain or by walking on wet soil and can be broken up by hoeing or lightly forking the surface. See also *pan*.

Carbonate of lime A manufactured powdered form of calcium carbonate derived from chalk or limestone.

Chalk A soft, white limestone derived from the skeletal remains of sea creatures. It can be present in the soil as parent material, and can increase the alkalinity of a soil.

Clay Soil particles which are 0.002mm or less in diameter (see appendix). They bind strongly to water and nutrients.

Clay soil Predominantly made of clay, it swells and feels sticky when wet and shrinks and cracks when dry. It moulds easily together when you squeeze it in your hand and is referred to as a cold and heavy soil. It holds on to water but gives little away to plants and is prone to waterlogging. Many nutrients are locked up in clay soil but it can be made fertile with intense cultivation and treatment with lime and organic matter.

Coarse sand Large particles of sand between 0.2mm and 2mm in diameter (see appendix).

Cold soil Soil which does not warm up very quickly, and when it does, it loses the heat easily. This is because it contains more water than air pockets. Clay soils are referred to as cold.

Compaction The result of compacting the soil too much either naturally by heavy rainfall or by treading on the soil especially if it is wet. The crumb structure is damaged as air is driven out but this is rectified by the incorporation of coarse materials and digging.

Crumb structure A good soil structure because it is broken up into small 'crumbs' from about 2mm to 20mm in diameter and neither gets waterlogged nor dries out too fast. The crumbs have space between them so that roots can penetrate easily and water can percolate deeper into the soil. Each crumb is made up of finer particles which hold onto the maximum amount of water for optimum plant growth and allows the rest to drain away. Gardeners aim to produce a good crumb structure by forking, adding organic matter, providing good drainage, creating little compaction and digging in the autumn so that the elements can break down the clods over winter. It is important to note that over-cultivation can destroy the crumb structure.

Cultivated soil Refers to soil which has been tended by a gardener rather than left to its own devices. It infers that the gardener has broken up the soil, incorporated organic matter and/or grown plants on it.

Decomposition The breakdown or decay of organic matter by means of soil organisms which use oxygen.

Denitrification The conversion of nitrates into atmospheric nitrogen and ammonia. This can be done by bacteria, especially in waterlogged soils, and is detrimental to soil fertility and plant health.

Drainage The passage of water through the soil. The ability of the soil to allow water to pass through it is predominantly affected by soil structure and texture and can be altered by levels of organic matter, soil organisms and cultivation.

Earthworm An animal that lives in the soil, mixes plant matter into the soil and improves aeration. Earthworms are beneficial in compost heaps, and beds and borders but are a nuisance in lawns as they leave their worm-casts on the surface on which weeds can grow. Earthworms can also be a problem if they enter pots containing plants as they make the soil or compost hard and reduce it to a poor structure.

Fallow Unplanted, uncultivated or rested soil. A soil is left fallow for any amount of time in order to redress the balance of nutrients or to allow soil with major pest, disease or weed problems to be treated.

Fertile soil A soil in which most plants will thrive due to the balance of available nutrients. Soil can be rated by the amount of organic matter that it contains and fertile soil is said to have between 2% and 7% organic matter present. Visibly, a fertile soil will be brown in colour and friable.

Fine sand Small particles of sand between 0.02mm and 0.2mm in diameter (see appendix).

Flocculation The process whereby soil particles bind together to form larger particles, thus improving the crumb structure. In clay soil this is achieved by adding lime which causes the clay particles to attach themselves around the lime particles.

Free-draining soil See *well-drained soil*.

Friable Describes a soil which is easy to crumble and is neither too wet nor too dry. Friable soil can produce a good tilth.

Fungus (*singular*) **fungi** (*plural*) Soil organisms which are primitive plants without chlorophyll so cannot photosynthesise.

They rely on organic matter for their energy and carbon. Fungi can be saprophytic, feeding on dead organic matter, or parasitic, feeding on living organisms, or symbiotic where a mutually beneficial relationship occurs between the fungus and the living organism.

Gravel Soil particles which are roughly between 2mm and 20mm in diameter. They are weathered pieces of rock and do not bind strongly to water or nutrients.

Heavy soil A loose term to describe soil which has relatively more clay particles and is heavier or harder to dig.

Humification The process whereby organic matter is decomposed into humus by fungi, bacteria and earthworms in an aerobic soil.

Humus Organic matter which has been broken down by fungi, bacteria and earthworms into a dark brown, almost black substance. The most important factor in this process is the availability of oxygen which ensures complete decomposition into very small particles. Humus increases soil temperature, absorbs water and contains nutrients, particularly nitrogen, and so is a source of food for plants and micro-organisms. Most importantly it binds soil particles making sandy soils more moisture-retentive and clay soils more aerated, thus improving the crumb structure.

Hungry soil One which does not contain readily-available nutrients or loses them rapidly and easily, and so requires large amounts of organic matter or fertilisers.

Hydrated lime/slaked lime A manufactured form of calcium hydroxide, which is a chemical compound of calcium, oxygen and hydrogen.

Hyphae Microscopic thread-like structures which make up the mycelium in fungi and spread out to find food.

Indicator weed A weed which grows and thrives on a particular type of soil or pH level, so that the gardener can make a rough assumption of the soil type and pH level.

Infertile soil A soil that lacks the essential nutrients for the growth of most plants. A soil may be infertile due to the soil type, lack of organic matter, over-cultivation or leaching of nutrients.

Leaching   The loss of minerals and nutrients from the soil due to heavy rainfall or irrigation. The type of soil and the amount of organic matter within the soil affect leaching.

Light soil   A loose term to describe soil which has relatively more sand particles and is lighter or easier to dig.

Lime   In horticulture, lime describes a number of calcium compounds which raise the soil pH. Examples are hydrated or slaked lime and carbonate of lime.

Liming   Incorporating lime into the soil to help neutralise acidity, to enhance the activity of soil organisms, to influence the availability of certain soil nutrients or to improve the crumb structure of clay soils.

Loam   A type of soil which contains a mixture of sand, silt and clay particles. A good garden loam will contain 40% sand, 30% silt and 30% clay and can occur naturally or can be bought.

Marling   Incorporating crushed limestone into the soil for the same reasons as liming, although this method is rarely used now as it is labour-intensive and expensive.

Mineral   The inorganic part of the soil derived from rock which has been weathered into varying sizes of particles. Minerals include sand, silt and clay. The type and quantity of minerals in the soil also determine which nutrients are available.

Moist soil   A soil which holds on to water between the soil particles but still allows air pockets to exist so that it is not saturated.

Moulds   A group of fungi which have microscopic hyphae and are vigorous in the decomposition of organic matter in any pH of soil, especially acid soil. In most cases they are more important than mushroom fungi and bacteria in this process.

Mushroom fungi A group of fungi that have an extensive mass of hyphae and bear fruiting bodies above ground. They are found in soils which are moist and have ample organic matter, especially woodland and grassland. They are important in the breakdown of woody material.

Mycelium   The main body of a fungus which consists of branched root-like structures which smell mushroomy or mouldy.

Mycorrhiza   Meaning 'fungus root' it refers to certain fungi that have a symbiotic relationship with the roots of plants. Mycorrhiza penetrate the roots of plants to obtain food and in return these fungi provide an enhanced availability of nutrients to the plant. This relationship has been observed in many trees, heath plants and grasses and is important particularly on infertile soil.

Neutral soil   Soil which is neutral (as opposed to acid or alkaline) because it has a medium concentration of hydrogen ions and ranges from pH4.5 to pH8.5. Alkaline soil can be made more neutral by the incorporation of peat compost, pine needles or pine bark. Conversely, acid soil can be made more neutral by liming or marling.

Nitrification   The conversion of atmospheric nitrogen and ammonia into nitrates (a useful form which plants can absorb). This is done by nitrogen-fixing bacteria and to a much lesser extent by lightning.

Nitrogen cycle   The sequence of chemical and biological changes of nitrogen as it moves from the atmosphere into water, soil and living organisms, and when these organisms die, it moves through a part or all of this process again.

Nitrogen fixing/nitrogen fixation   The process by which some bacteria, rhizobia, convert nitrogen gas into nitrates, which can be utilised by plants.

Nutrient   A chemical element derived from the mineral particles in the soil. Nutrients are essential for plant growth and are used to form cell components, to act as catalysts in chemical reactions and also to maintain chemical balances in the plant. Plant nutrients are divided into two groups, major elements and trace elements. Nutrients may exist in the soil in a chemical form that is unavailable to the plants, so chemical reactions need to take place and the nutrient needs to become soluble before the plant can absorb it.

Organic matter   Material derived from living or dead organisms (plants or animals) which contains carbon compounds. Fresh organic matter accumulates on the soil surface and is gradually pulled down into the soil, making it more open. This allows water and air to penetrate and so improves the soil structure. Organic matter which has been decomposed by fungi, bacteria and earthworms turns into humus depending upon the aeration, moisture and temperature within the soil. Organic matter is also important for soil fertility as it contains varying amounts of nutrients. Organic matter can be naturally present in the soil or be introduced by gardeners in the form of compost, manure or mulch.

Oxidation The breakdown of humus by oxygen into carbon dioxide and water. This means that humus is rapidly lost from sandy soils because they are highly aerobic. Conversely, waterlogged soils are anaerobic so humus builds up in deep layers.

Pan A hard horizontal layer of soil either on top of the soil or beneath the surface through which roots cannot grow. A surface pan, or cap, is produced by compaction after heavy rain or by walking on wet soil and can be broken up by hoeing or lightly forking the surface. A sub-surface pan is caused by cultivating to the same depth over a long period and can be broken up by double digging.

Parent material Partly weathered rock beneath the subsoil. This has little or no organic matter so is infertile.

Peat soil A soil with a high quantity of undecomposed organic matter which becomes compressed under its own weight. It contains little or no available nutrients. Soil can be rated by the amount of organic matter that it contains and peat soils are said to have between 20% and 95% organic matter present. Visibly, peat soil is almost black in colour.

pH From the word 'power' and the chemical symbol for 'hydrogen'. pH is a measure of the concentration of hydrogen ions and therefore a measure of acidity and alkalinity. The pH scale ranges from pH0 which is acidic, to pH14 which is alkaline, with pH7 being neutral. It is a logarithmic scale so that the next number up the scale is ten times more alkaline than the previous number. Most soils within the UK lie within the range of pH4.5 and pH8.5. pH6.5 is the optimum level for the majority of plants as it has the widest range of nutrients available (see appendix).

Poor soil Soil which is infertile and/or has a poor structure. It can be improved by cultivation techniques.

Protozoan (*singular*) **protozoa** (*plural*) Microscopic soil organisms which feed on bacteria so can potentially decrease decomposition. They are often found in a soil which has had one crop continuously grown on it and can be removed by soil sterilisation.

Rhizobium (*singular*) **rhizobia** (*plural*) Certain bacteria which live symbiotically with plants, in the root nodules of legumes. They receive food from the plant and, because they convert atmospheric nitrogen into forms that the plant can take up, they benefit the plant's health and generally increase soil fertility.

Rich soil   A soil which contains high levels of available nutrients. Soil can be rated by the amount of organic matter that it contains and rich soil is said to have between 7% and 15% organic matter present. Visibly, a rich soil will be dark brown in colour and the organic matter will be a mix of undecomposed and decomposed material.

Sand   Soil particles which are between 0.02mm and 2mm in diameter (see appendix). They are unweathered pieces of rock and do not bind strongly to water or nutrients.

Sandy soil   Predominantly made of sand, it feels gritty when wet and is loose when dry. It does not mould together when you squeeze it in your hand and is referred to as a warm and light soil. It is well aerated and free-draining but nutrients can leach out and water can evaporate easily. Sandy soils require little cultivation other than the application of organic matter and frequent feeding.

Saprophytic   Describes certain fungi and bacteria that live on dead and decaying organic matter. They aid the decomposition process and are vital in the formation of humus. Moulds and mushroom fungi are both examples of saprophytic fungi.

Shallow soil   Soil which has a thin layer of topsoil above the subsoil.

Silt   Soil particles which are between 0.002mm and 0.02mm in diameter (see appendix). They have water and nutrient-holding properties between sand and clay.

Silty soil   Predominantly made of silt, it feels silky but not sticky and the particles pack together when squeezed in the hand to form crumbs. It holds on to a fair amount of water but equally has good drainage. Nutrients are readily available to plants in silty soils so fertility is quite high. It can have compaction problems and form pans after heavy rain so moderate cultivation may be needed (see appendix).

Slaked lime   See *hydrated lime.*

Soil   A mixture of five main constituents which may vary in quantity. These constituents are inorganic material (rock minerals), organic material (dead and decaying plants and animals), water, air and living organisms (including fungi, bacteria and earthworms).

Soil analysis   A test done on a sample of soil to determine its chemical components and pH level. Thorough soil tests also include the analysis of the type of soil particles and can indicate any nutrient deficiencies. Soil analysis can often detect certain fungal and bacterial diseases as well. It is best to provide more than one soil sample from different areas in the garden to get a full picture as soil conditions can change dramatically within as short a distance as one metre.

Soil organism   An organism which lives in the soil. These organisms exist in their millions and influence soil fertility, aeration and drainage. Beneficial soil organisms are algae, saprophytic and symbiotic fungi, aerobic bacteria, most eelworms, earthworms and some insects. Detrimental soil organisms are parasitic fungi, anaerobic bacteria, protozoa, and some eelworms and insects.

Soil profile   A cross-section of soil sliced downwards to include the topsoil, subsoil, parent material and bedrock.

Soil structure   The way in which the constituents of the soil are organised into larger particles or crumbs. The structure influences the availability of oxygen, water and nutrients to the plant and the ability of the roots to penetrate the soil. Soil structure is not fixed but changes over time with weathering and can also be modified by the gardener by cultivation.

Soil texture   The composition of the soil defined by the size of soil particles. In the garden you can rub soil between your fingers to determine the general texture. A clay soil will feel sticky, a silty soil will feel silky and a sandy soil will feel gritty.

Sour	An acid soil can be referred to as sour.
Subsoil	The layer below the topsoil which contains less organic matter and has fewer soil organisms so is fairly infertile. It is characteristically lighter in colour than the topsoil and can be wet and sticky in the winter and dry and hard during the summer.
Sweeten	Decreasing soil acidity, usually by adding lime.
Symbiotic	Describes a mutually beneficial relationship between two living organisms. Rhizobia are examples of symbiotic bacteria and mycorrhiza are examples of symbiotic fungi.
Topsoil	The top layer of soil which contains the plant roots, organic matter, micro-organisms and nutrients. Topsoil should have a good structure and be dark in colour. It can vary in depth from a few centimetres to one metre and, if it is very shallow, further topsoil can be added with the same texture and pH as the existing soil.
Warm soil	Soil which warms up more rapidly and retains the heat for longer because it contains more air pockets than water. Sandy soils are referred to as warm.
Water table	The upper level of groundwater below which the soil is saturated with water. The water table can rise after periods of prolonged heavy rain, and if it reaches the soil surface it causes flooding. Similarly, it can fall after periods of drought.
Waterlogged	Soil that is saturated with water.
Well-drained soil/free-draining soil	A soil which allows water to pass through it with ease.

Soil
improvement

Activator   A product that contains bacteria or high nitrogen sources which can be added to a compost pile in order to start the decomposition process. It can be obtained in granule form and is applied at a measured rate for size of the compost pile. It is not an essential ingredient and an alternative is to sprinkle a thin layer of garden soil or manure into the compost pile.

Bark   An organic material made from chipped and sterilised bark from trees. It is mainly used as an ornamental mulch but it can also be incorporated into the soil to improve aeration. Bacteria use nitrogen to decompose the bark so this method can leave the soil short of nitrogen. Bark contains virtually no nutrients and is relatively expensive.

Biodegradeable   A material which is capable of being decomposed by soil organisms.

Carboniferous   Technically, any material containing carbon. In horticulture, woody or brown material that is used for composting is referred to as carboniferous (as opposed to soft and green). These compost ingredients can include prunings from trees and shrubs, dry leaves, straw and wood shavings.

Coco shells   A by-product from the coconut industry. The shells are chipped and sterilised and can be used as an organic and ornamental mulch.

Compost   The end result of composting, a humus-rich soil. Good compost is brown and crumbly and should have a soil-like aroma. It is neither too wet nor completely dry and the organic components should not be identifiable because they have been thoroughly broken down. Compost can be used in the garden as a mulch, or forked into the soil as a soil conditioner or mixed with other materials to form a growing medium for container-grown plants. It is also a source of nutrients.

Compost activator See *activator*.

Compost bin An enclosed compost heap. Plastic dustbins can be used with a few alterations such as removing the base so the heap sits on the soil surface, and creating holes in the sides to improve aeration. The bin can also be made out of wooden slats or four wooden pallets nailed together. Alternatively, a length of wire fencing can be coiled into a cylinder and secured. There are also a number of commercial, usually plastic, bins that can be obtained.

Compost heap A simple pile of organic materials mixed together and placed directly on the ground. The pile needs to be at least one metre tall at its highest point in order to create enough heat for rapid decomposition. Materials can be gradually added until the heap is large enough although it is better to build the heap in one go to create enough heat for rapid decomposition.

Composting The manual process or gardening activity of turning fresh organic matter into compost. Anything that is entirely organic can be composted except diseased material, woody material which is too large unless it is chipped or shredded, and cooked food or dead animals which can attract vermin. The organic matter is mixed or layered on a heap or in a bin and is decomposed by fungi, bacteria and earthworms. It is essential to ensure oxygen is present by providing ventilation or by turning the heap regularly. The heap must be watered at first and then covered for insulation and to prevent the compost getting too wet. It is also important to ensure a good mix of woody and green material to encourage a variety of soil organisms and to create air pockets. The natural process of composting is called humification.

Cool composting Making garden compost by simply piling organic matter into a heap and waiting for it to decompose. Materials are gradually added until the heap is large enough so it does not create enough heat for rapid decomposition. Therefore, it can take a year or more to be ready but requires little management.

Decomposition The breakdown of green and woody waste into humus or compost by bacteria, fungi and other soil organisms which utilise water and oxygen to achieve this.

Gravel   A mixture of coarse sand and pounded or water-worn stones which are roughly between 2mm and 20mm in diameter. They do not bind strongly to water or nutrients, and gravel is used to improve aeration and drainage in a soil. It is also used as an ornamental mulch, especially around alpines and plants which do not like being wet around the crown.

Green manure A crop which is grown on an empty plot of land specifically to be dug into the ground to add organic matter and improve the soil structure. It is usually grown over winter and dug in in the spring. Whilst the plants are growing they also suppress weeds, break up the soil and improve drainage. Bacteria use nitrogen to decompose the green manure so this method can leave the soil short of nitrogen. Good plants, therefore, for green manures are from the Leguminoseae family, such as broad beans, which can fix nitrogen in the soil.

Hot composting The best way to compost, it takes a little more effort but the result is much quicker. The heap is built in one go and the floor dimension must be a minimum of one square metre in order to create enough heat for rapid decomposition. The heap is started on the soil surface to allow soil organisms to enter the compost although the four sides are usually enclosed by a material with ventilation slits or holes. It is then built by adding layers, about 15cm deep, of different materials, and it is usual to alternate between nitrogenous and carboniferous materials. Thin layers of manure, soil or an activator can be added to introduce soil organisms. The heap is then watered and covered to prevent it getting too soggy from rain, and it should then be turned once a month or so to mix the materials and create adequate ventilation. Three heaps are often employed, one to receive incoming organic matter, one which is actively decomposing to which nothing is added, and one that is finished and ready to use as a mulch or soil conditioner. Compost will be ready in about three months during the summer or six months during the winter using this method.

Humification The natural process where organic matter on the soil surface is decomposed into humus by fungi, bacteria and earthworms. The most important factor in this process is the availability of oxygen which ensures the complete decomposition into very small particles. Humification is also dependent on the moisture and temperature within the soil. The manual process of humification is called composting.

Humus Organic matter which has been broken down by fungi, bacteria and earthworms into a dark brown, almost black substance. Humus increases soil temperature, absorbs water and contains nutrients, particularly nitrogen and so is a source of energy for plants and micro-organisms. Most importantly it binds soil particles making sandy soils more moisture-retentive and clay soils more aerated, thus improving the crumb structure.

Inorganic Material which is not derived from living or dead organisms (plants or animals) but is made from minerals and/or man-made materials.

Kitchen waste Fruit, vegetables, peelings, paper towels, egg shells, spent tea bags and ground coffee, etc. Cooked food or meat should not be put onto a compost heap as it will attract vermin and not smell too good. Kitchen waste is classed as nitrogenous or green material when added to the compost heap.

Leaf mould Leaves which have decomposed into a crumbly compost which can be used as a mulch, soil conditioner or mixed with other materials to make a potting compost. Leaves are decomposed predominantly by fungi, and not bacteria, so the leaf pile needs sunlight. Leaf mould can take up to two or three years to completely decompose, although it is usually ready for use after one year.

Lime In horticulture, lime describes a number of calcium compounds. Incorporating lime into a soil helps to neutralise acidity, enhance the activity of soil organisms, influence the availability of certain soil nutrients and improve the crumb structure of clay soils.

Manure/chicken manure/farmyard manure/horse manure Waste from animals such as cows, horses, pigs, sheep and chickens.

It is the best source of organic matter for a soil conditioner and also contains nutrients so is a good organic feed. Manure must be well-rotted before it is applied to the soil so that it does not scorch young shoots and roots. Also, because bacteria utilise nitrogen to decompose the manure, it can leave the soil short of nitrogen.

Mulch   A layer of material placed on the soil surface to conserve soil moisture, suppress weeds, reduce soil temperature fluctuations, and protect the soil from erosion and capping. It can also be ornamental. Inorganic materials used as a mulch include polythene, old carpets, weed control fabric or gravel. These usually form a thin layer and are used just as a mulch which remains on the soil surface. Organic materials used as a mulch include bark, compost, coco shells or straw. These usually form a thick layer from about 5cm to 15cm in depth on the soil surface but eventually will be worked into the soil. Mulch is usually applied from autumn to spring but can also be used during the growing season as long as the soil surface is moist prior to application.

Nitrogenous   Technically, any material containing nitrogen. In horticulture, material that is used for composting is referred to as nitrogenous if it is soft and green, for example, grass clippings or kitchen waste, as opposed to woody.

Organic   Describes material derived from living or dead organisms (plants or animals) which all contain carbon compounds. Organic soil improvement not only means using organic materials instead of inorganic chemicals, it also involves mimicking nature's recycling processes by actively replacing what is taken out of the soil.

Organic matter   Material derived from living or dead organisms (plants or animals) which contain carbon compounds. Fresh organic matter accumulates on the soil

> **TOP TIP**
>
> **When applying a mulch around plants**
> Ensure that there is a space between the material and the stems of woody plants so that it does not encourage rot.

surface and is gradually pulled down into the soil, or it can be collected and composted and used as a soil conditioner or mulch. Organic matter makes the soil more open, allowing water and air to penetrate and so improving the soil structure. It is also important for soil fertility as it contains varying degrees of nutrients.

Peat An organic soil conditioner which is used to improve soil structure and moisture retention. It has virtually no nutrients. Alternatives to peat are now being found and used due to the destruction of rare habitats during the harvesting of the peat.

Seaweed An organic soil conditioner found washed-up on beaches. It is excellent for improving the soil structure as it binds the particles together. It is also a source of nutrients, particularly potassium, and is rich in the full range of trace elements. It is a good compost activator as it attracts aerobic bacteria which decompose organic matter.

Sheet composting Applying a layer of fresh organic matter as a mulch rather than composting it first. The material will decompose naturally over time and be drawn down into the soil improving the structure. Bacteria use the nitrogen in the soil to decompose the material so this method can leave the soil short of nitrogen. It is still a useful method in small gardens when there is not enough room for a compost heap or when only small amounts of waste material are removed from the garden or produced in the kitchen.

Soil conditioner/soil improver Anything that is incorporated into the soil to improve it or change the way it behaves. Organic matter is the most effective soil conditioner, for example, compost, manure, leaf mould, spent compost, spent materials, seaweed, peat, coco shells and bark chips. A conditioner improves the soil

> TOP TIP
>
> **If you have a local horse-riding school**
> Many stables will let you have free manure if you pick it up yourself. Make sure you get the well-rotted stuff and also check that they use straw or peat as bedding because wood shavings can be a source of disease.

structure because it is bulky which improves aeration and more importantly it binds soil particles together and absorbs water which increases the moisture-holding capacity of the soil. This makes sandy soils more moisture-retentive and opens up clay soils. A conditioner can also increase the soil temperature. It can introduce micro-organisms and nutrients, particularly nitrogen, so increases soil fertility. Soil conditioners are usually dug or forked into the soil during autumn but can applied as a mulch and allowed to be naturally worked into the soil. Inorganic materials such as lime or gravel can improve the condition of a soil by encouraging flocculation and aeration. The terms soil conditioner and soil improver are used interchangeably.

Spent compost Any compost that has been used in pots for seeds, cuttings or plants and is turned out when the plants are potted on. Home-made spent compost should ideally be sterilised before using as a mulch, a top dressing on lawns or a soil conditioner, so that pests and diseases are not spread throughout the garden.

Spent hops An organic material obtained from breweries after the hops have been utilised in the brewing process. It is mainly used as a soil conditioner but also contains a small amount of nutrients, particularly phosphorus.

Spent mushroom compost An organic material obtained from mushroom growers once the mushrooms have been harvested. It is made up of horse manure, peat and chalk although this mixture may vary. It is incorporated into the soil as a conditioner but it can be slightly alkaline so is not used around calcifuge plants. It is also a source of the nutrients nitrogen, phosphorus and potassium, and the full range of trace elements.

Turf stack A good way to recycle old lawn by stacking the turf on top of one another. Every other turf is turned upside down so that the soil sides are next to each other and the grass sides are too. It can take a year or so for it to decompose but the result is a good alternative to topsoil.

Nutrients and fertilisers

Ammonia A compound containing hydrogen and nitrogen, which in a soluble form can be absorbed by plants.

Ammonium nitrate An inorganic fertiliser which is a source of nitrogen. It is readily soluble and is applied in a liquid or granule formulation early in the season.

Ammonium sulphate See *sulphate of ammonia.*

Balanced fertiliser/general fertiliser A fertiliser that contains more than one major nutrient and usually contains roughly equal percentages of nitrogen, phosphorus and potassium.

Base dressing Fertiliser which is applied to the soil prior to planting, either at the bottom of a planting hole and therefore at the base of the roots, or incorporated into the soil during preparation. A base dressing is an initial feed as opposed to a top dressing.

Bonemeal An organic fertiliser which contains a form of phosphorus that plants can absorb. It also contains nitrogen but most of this is removed in the sterilisation process. It is made from crushed animal bone and is applied as a powder. It is used as a base dressing and, because it releases the nutrient slowly, it can remain in the soil for three to four years.

Boron (B) A trace element and nutrient which is present in small amounts in the soil. Plants use soluble forms of boron for a number of processes including the transport of sugars and uptake of calcium, although plant usage of boron is not well understood. Boron may be unavailable to plants on sandy soil and uptake may be low in calcium-rich soil.

Calcium (Ca) A major element and nutrient which is abundant in most soils, especially those derived from chalk or limestone, although acid soils lack sufficient calcium for most plants. Plants use soluble forms of calcium particularly in the construction of cell walls.

Calcium carbonate A white insoluble chemical compound which occurs naturally as chalk or limestone. Manufactured forms are sometimes referred to as carbonate of lime. It is a source of the nutrient calcium as well as helping to reduce soil acidity or improve the crumb structure of clay soils.

Carbonate of lime A manufactured powdered form of calcium carbonate derived from chalk or limestone.

Chicken manure See *manure*.

Comfrey The Russian species of this herbaceous perennial plant can be grown and the leaves harvested for a compost high in potassium and containing trace elements. It can also be used to produce an organic liquid fertiliser in a compost bin with a tap at the base.

Controlled-release fertiliser See *slow-release fertiliser*.

Copper (Cu) A trace element and nutrient present in the soil. Plants use copper in small amounts as part of important enzymes involved in chemical reactions. Excessive phosphates can reduce copper availability.

Deficiency The lack of one or more of the nutrients in a soil. Also describes the disorder that the plant shows because of the lack of the relevant nutrient, for example, manganese deficiency.

Dried blood An organic fertiliser which contains a form of nitrogen that plants can absorb. It quickly releases the nutrient so tends to be used as a one-off application for nitrogen deficiency, and it is also expensive so is mainly used for established greenhouse and pot plants.

Epsom salts An inorganic fertiliser which is a source of magnesium in the form of magnesium sulphate and is commonly used as a liquid feed. The name refers to the town of Epsom in Surrey, where magnesium sulphate was first found occurring naturally.

Farmyard manure See *manure*.

Feed The action of applying a fertiliser to a plant. The term is also used interchangeably with the term fertiliser.

Fertiliser A manufactured and concentrated source of a plant nutrient or nutrients. A fertiliser is used to replace or increase nutrients which are lost due to the removal of vegetation or leaching out by rain. A fertiliser can be organic or inorganic, may supply one or more nutrients in varying ratios, can be applied to the soil or to the leaves of the plant and can release the nutrients immediately or gradually over a period.

Fish, blood and bone An organic fertiliser which contains forms of nitrogen, phosphorus and potassium that plants can absorb. The components are dried and crushed and it is applied as a powder. The size of the particles determines the rate at which the nutrients are released. It is considered a good organic alternative to a balanced fertiliser although the ratios of nutrients can vary and it is often low in phosphorus and nitrogen.

Foliar feed/foliar spray Fertiliser which is applied as a liquid spray to the leaves of a plant. The nutrients are absorbed by the leaves and distributed throughout the plant. It is usually a one-off application in order to correct a deficiency.

General fertiliser See *balanced fertiliser*.

Green manure A crop which is grown on an empty plot of land specifically to be dug into the ground to add organic matter and nutrients. It is usually grown over winter and dug in in the spring. Whilst the crop is growing it also suppresses weeds, breaks up the soil and improves drainage. Good plants for green manures are from the Leguminoseae family, such as broad beans, which can fix nitrogen in the soil.

Growmore An inorganic balanced fertiliser with an equal NPK ratio. Although it is a trade name it is also used generically.

Hoof and horn An organic fertiliser which contains a form of nitrogen that plants can absorb. It is made from crushed hooves and horns from certain animals and the nitrogen is released by soil bacteria. It is usually applied as a base dressing and is also found in John Innes potting composts.

Horse manure See *manure*.

Inorganic fertiliser One which is derived from rock sources or produced artificially by chemical manufacture.

Iron (Fe)　A trace element and plant nutrient present in the soil. Plants use iron in small amounts for a number of processes such as respiration and also for the production of chlorophyll. Iron may be unavailable to plants on alkaline soil.

Liquid feed　Fertiliser which is either diluted in water or ready-made in liquid form. It is applied to the soil around plants and is commonly used for feeding plants in containers.

Magnesium (Mg)　A major element and plant nutrient which is derived from rock. Plants use magnesium in large amounts for many processes, especially in the production of chlorophyll. It is important to note that magnesium and potassium adversely affect each other's uptake by the plant, and calcium reduces magnesium availability.

Magnesium sulphate　An inorganic fertiliser which is a source of magnesium. It is soluble and is commonly used as a liquid feed.

Major element　A nutrient which is needed by plants in large amounts. Nitrogen, phosphorus, and potassium are the three main major elements used by plants, and magnesium, calcium and sulphur are also classified as major elements.

Manganese (Mn)　A trace element and nutrient which is present in the soil. Plants use soluble forms of manganese for a number of chemical reactions including respiration and photosynthesis. Manganese may be unavailable to plants on chalky soil or soil with high amounts of organic matter.

Manure/chicken manure/farmyard manure/horse manure　An organic source of many nutrients although the amounts can vary considerably. It is the waste from animals such as cows, horses, pigs, sheep and chickens. It is also the best source of organic matter for a soil conditioner. Manure must be well-rotted before it is applied to the soil so that it does not scorch young shoots and roots, and, because bacteria utilise nitrogen to decompose the manure, it can leave the soil short of nitrogen.

Mineral　The inorganic part of the soil derived from rock which has been weathered into varying sizes of particles.

Minerals include sand, silt and clay. The type and quantity of minerals in the soil also determine which nutrient elements are available.

Molybdenum (Mo) A trace element and nutrient which is present in the soil. Plants use soluble forms of molybdenum and it is particularly important for nitrogen fixation. It is readily available to plants in alkaline soil but may be deficient in acid soil.

Muriate of potash An inorganic fertiliser which is a source of potassium. It contains potassium chloride and is rarely used in greenhouses or on fruit and vegetables because it can lead to a build-up of chlorine in the soil.

Nitrate A compound containing oxygen and nitrogen, which in a soluble form can be absorbed by plants.

Nitrate of potash An inorganic fertiliser which is a source of potassium. It contains potassium nitrate which is very soluble and is used widely in liquid feeds.

Nitrochalk An inorganic fertiliser that is a source of nitrogen and calcium. It contains ammonium nitrate and calcium carbonate (chalk). The presence of chalk helps to neutralise soil acidity and it is often added to peat-based composts.

Nitrogen (N) A major element and nutrient which is converted from the air and soil by bacteria into nitrates. Plants use soluble forms of nitrogen for many processes, especially vegetative growth and making chlorophyll. Nitrogen is easily lost from the soil by leaching.

Nitrogen-fixing/nitrogen fixation The process by which rhizobia convert nitrogen gas into nitrates, which can be utilised by plants.

NPK ratio The letters N, P and K are the chemical symbols for nitrogen, phosphorus and potassium respectively. Balanced fertiliser labels indicate the ratios of these three major elements. The appropriate fertiliser can then be selected depending upon the time of year, the specific requirements of the plant, a nutrient deficiency which needs to be rectified, or to encourage a developmental stage in the plant.

Nutrient A chemical element which is essential for healthy plant growth. All nutrients are essential although may be required in varying amounts. Nutrients are obtained from the soil by the plant's root hairs and are then used to help build cells, to control chemical reactions or to maintain chemical balances within the plant. When a plant dies it decomposes and the nutrients are recycled in the soil and become available again. Plant nutrients are divided into major elements and trace elements.

Nutrient deficiency See *deficiency*.

Organic fertiliser One which is derived from plant or animal sources. The nutrient content may be variable and the fertiliser may also contain some inorganic chemicals but this should be stated on the label. Organic fertilisers can be slow to release the nutrients but this is largely dependent upon the water content and temperature of the soil.

Osmocote An inorganic balanced fertiliser usually available in prill formulation. It is a slow-release fertiliser and although it is a trade name it is also used generically.

Phosphate A compound containing oxygen and phosphorus, which in a soluble form can be absorbed by plants.

Phosphorus (P) A major element and nutrient which is present in the soil and is converted by soil bacteria into a phosphate which plants can absorb. Plants use phosphorus in large amounts for many processes. It is important mainly for root formation but also for early ripening and maturity of fruit, and young plants need high amounts. Phosphorus is not always available to the plant, especially in acid and clay soils.

Potash An inorganic fertiliser which is a source of potassium. It contains either potassium carbonate or potassium hydroxide. The term is derived from the archaic practice of obtaining a form of potassium by leaching wood and vegetable ashes and then evaporating the solution in pots, literally, pot-ashes.

Potassium (K) A major element and nutrient which is present in the soil. Plants use soluble forms of potassium for many processes and it is particularly important for flower and fruit production and disease resistance. Potassium is easily leached and rapidly depleted especially on light or sandy soils. It is also important to note that potassium and magnesium adversely affect each other's uptake by the plant, and calcium reduces potassium availability.

Prill A formulation of fertiliser which is a small sphere contained within a protective coating through which the fertiliser is released.

Quick-release fertiliser Fertiliser that is or can be soluble allowing the plant roots to take up the nutrients easily and quickly, for example, liquid feed.

Salts In horticulture, the term 'salts' generally refers to any nutrients in the soil that a plant can absorb.

Scorch A disorder where the foliage dries out and turns brown either due to excessive sunlight, especially after watering in sunny weather, or fertiliser or pesticide applications which have wetted the leaves. Scorch can also affect the roots if an overdose of fertiliser or pesticide is given, or if applications are made when the soil is too dry.

Seaweed An organic fertiliser which contains forms of nitrogen, phosphorus and potassium that plants can absorb, but is mainly a source of trace elements. It is applied in a powdered form as a base dressing, or as a liquid feed.

Sequestered A metallic ion, bound so that it cannot react further. For example, iron is applied as a fertiliser in sequestered form so that it does not react with oxygen and water.

Slow-release fertiliser/controlled-release fertiliser Fertiliser which gradually becomes available for uptake by the plant roots over a long period. The nutrients become available in the soil by chemical reactions to water and heat or by the action of soil organisms. It is usually available as coated granules or prills and most organic fertilisers are also slow-release. This formulation closely mimics the natural nutrient availability in the soil, and is also beneficial because fewer applications are needed to cover the growing season of the plant.

Soluble Describes a solid substance which can be dissolved in water. Plants can only absorb soluble fertilisers or nutrients.

Sulphate   A compound containing oxygen and sulphur, which in a soluble form can be absorbed by plants.

Sulphate of ammonia An inorganic fertiliser which is a source of nitrogen in the form of ammonium sulphate. It is very soluble and is usually applied to young plants early in the season.

Sulphate of potash An inorganic fertiliser which is a source of potassium in the form of potassium sulphate. It is used in greenhouses but can cause calcium deficiency if excessive amounts are used.

Sulphur (S)   A major element and nutrient which is present in mineral particles in the soil. Plants use soluble forms of sulphur for specialised processes such as forming proteins and other compounds.

Superphosphate An inorganic fertiliser which is a source of phosphorus. It contains calcium phosphate and calcium sulphate and is widely available as a powder or as granules. It is usually applied as a base dressing and is often a constituent of potting composts.

Top dressing   Fertiliser which is applied to the top of the soil and left to be washed in by water. A top dressing is normally scattered around plants in subsequent years after planting, as opposed to a base dressing.

Trace element A plant nutrient which is needed in small amounts. Manganese, iron, boron, zinc, copper and molybdenum are the trace elements.

Wormery   Normally a plastic bin with a tap at the bottom, preferably with three horizontal compartments separated by perforated boards or wire or plastic meshing. All kitchen waste is placed in the top compartment, with tiger worms and bedding in the second compartment. The lowest compartment drains the excess moisture. It is mainly designed to remove kitchen waste, but the worms do produce a small amount of compost and the excess moisture at the bottom can be used as an organic liquid feed.

Zinc (Zn)   A trace element and nutrient widely distributed in the soil. Plants use soluble forms of zinc in the build-up of auxin and protein. Zinc becomes less available on more neutral to alkaline soils.

Botany

Parts of plants

Achene   A small dry fruit which contains one seed and which does not split open to disperse the seed.

Adventitious root A root which grows from an unusual part of the plant rather than from the radicle or subsequent subdivisions of root. They can appear from stems or leaf axils and may or may not grow into the ground.

Aerial root   A root borne wholly above the ground either adventitously or from rooting axes in epiphytes.

Anther   The swollen tip of the stamen where pollen is produced and dispersed.

Apex   The tip of a root, shoot or leaf.

Axil   The angle between the stem and the leaf petiole.

Bark   Protective layer on the outside of woody stems made up of dead cells.

Berry   A fleshy fruit which contains more than one seed.

Blossom   The flower or mass of flowers on trees (especially fruit) and mainly referred to in spring.

Bract   A leaf-like structure on the flower stem which is often thought to be a petal when the flower itself is insignificant. The bracts may resemble leaves or be brightly coloured like petals.

Bud   An undeveloped shoot or flower on a stem which is protected by scales. An apical bud is at the tip of a shoot, a lateral bud is contained between the stem and leaf petiole and the terminal bud is at the tip of the leader or growing shoot at the top of the plant.

Bulb   A storage organ consisting of a compacted stem and fleshy leaves underground. It enables perennation and vegetative reproduction.

Bulbil   A small immature bulb usually attached to the parent bulb but they can also be produced in leaf axils or on the stem near a flowerhead.

Calyx   The circle of sepals which make up the outer whorl of a flower.

Cambium   The layer of actively dividing cells between the phloem and xylem. This forms a continuous layer beneath the bark in woody plants. The cambium constantly produces new cells so that the stem thickens in size.

Carpel   The female reproductive organ of a flower consisting of the stigma, style and ovary.

Cell   A living unit made up of a nucleus, vacuole and cytoplasm surrounded by a membrane.

Cell wall   The rigid wall inside the membrane surrounding a cell. It is made of cellulose and is fully permeable to water, sugars and nutrients.

Chlorophyll   The green pigment found in chloroplasts which helps determine the amount of photosynthesis that can occur.

Chloroplast   A structure found in the cytoplasm of leaf and stem cells. The chloroplasts contain chlorophyll and this is where photosynthesis occurs.

Chromosome   A thread-like structure found in the nucleus of all cells, which controls cell division. The chromosomes contain DNA and as a whole they control the development and characteristics of the plant.

Collar   See *crown*.

Compound leaf   A leaf which is divided into leaflets.

Cone   A cluster of dense scales which is the reproductive structure in gymnosperms. The hard cones are female and the scales usually open to release the seeds.

Cork   The rough layer beneath the bark on woody stems. It is made from dead cells and is impervious to water.

Corm   An underground storage organ consisting of a swollen stem base. It enables perennation and vegetative reproduction.

Corolla   The circle of petals which make up the inner whorl of a flower.

Cortex   The main body of cells in a root between the inner vascular systems and the epidermis. It regulates the passage of water and nutrients and food is stored here.

Cotyledon The first leaf, or leaves, of a plant which has stored food for the seed and become the initial photosynthetic organ for the germinated seedling. Also known as seed leaves.

Crown/collar/neck The upper part of the root ball where shoots arise, and conversely, the base of the stem where it joins the roots.

Culm The stem of grass.

Cuticle A waxy layer impermeable to water on the surface of leaves and stems.

Cytoplasm All parts of a cell outside the nucleus and inside the membrane which contain chloroplasts and mitochondria.

DNA Contained in the genes and it carries the genetic code for a particular characteristic of a cell or an organism.

Drupe A fruit where the seed is covered by a hard stony endocarp.

Embryo The whole of the plant at its earliest stage contained within the seed.

Endocarp The inner layer of tissue in a fruit which surrounds the seeds.

Epidermis The outer layer of cells in roots, stems and leaves which help maintain rigidity.

Exocarp The outer skin of a fruit.

Feather One year of vegetative growth.

Fibrous root A root system where several roots grow down at the same time at roughly the same size and laterals grow from them. There is no tap root.

Filament The stalk of the stamen which attaches the anther to the receptacle.

Floret An individual flower in a closely packed inflorescence.

Flower The reproductive structure in angiosperms. It consists of the carpel (the female organ), the stamen (the male organ) and the perianth. Generally known as the blossom of the plant.

> **TOP TIP**
>
> **Storing seed**
> Use empty photo film containers to collect and store seed.

Frond	The leaf of a palm or fern.
Fruit	The organ in angiosperms which contains a seed. The fruit is produced from the development of the ovary after fertilisation.
Gene	A length of DNA in a chromosome.
Heartwood	The inner part of the xylem which is unable to transport sap but acts as support for the stem, trunk or branch.
Hilum	The scar on a seed marking where it was attached to the ovary.
Honey-guide	Markings in the form of spots or lines on the petals which are said to guide insects to the nectaries in the flower. Some honey-guides are invisible to the human eye but interestingly can be seen under UV light.
Inflorescence	The whole flowering part of the plant. It can describe individual florets but more usually a group of florets comprising a flowerhead. It is also generally used to describe the arrangement of flowers on a stem (see appendix).
Internode	The space on a stem between two nodes.
Kernel	The seed in a drupe.
Lamina	The blade of a leaf.
Lateral	A side shoot or bud emanating from a larger stem.
Leader	The main stem of a plant from which laterals grow. Usually applies to the apex of that stem.
Leaf	A plant organ growing out from a stem consisting of a petiole (stalk), lamina (blade) and veins, and where the functions of photosynthesis and transpiration mainly take place.
Leaf margin	The edge of a leaf.
Lenticel	A pore on the surface of a stem for gas exchange.
Lignified stem	A stem that is woody in texture due to the deposition of lignin.
Lignin	A hardening material within the cell walls of woody tissues.
Membrane	The part of a cell which holds in the cell contents. It is thin, living and selectively permeable.

Meristem	The tissue in a plant which is actively growing due to cell division taking place. It is usually at the growing tip of the root and shoot (apical meristem) although in many monocotyledons it is at the base of the stem and leaves. This includes grasses, which is why a lawn continues to grow after mowing. Lateral meristem is found between the phloem and xylem tissues in roots and stems of dicotyledons and is also known as the cambium.
Mesocarp	The middle layer of tissue in a fruit between the exocarp and endocarp.
Micropyle	The opening in the coat of the ovule through which the pollen tube enters at fertilisation. It then appears as a minute hole at the tip of the seed.
Midrib	The central vein on a leaf which runs from the petiole to the leaf tip.
Mitochondria	A structure found in the cytoplasm of cells and this is where respiration and energy release occur.
Neck	See *crown*.
Nectar	A sugary liquid secreted by the nectaries. The scent of the nectar attracts pollinators to the flower, and the nectar itself provides food as a reward.
Nectary	A gland which secretes nectar from inside many flowers.
Node	The point on a stem from where leaves and lateral stems may grow. The node is usually slightly swollen before producing a bud.
Nucleus	The living part of a cell which controls cell activity.
Nut	A dry fruit with the seed contained within a hard shell (pericarp) which does not split open to disperse the seed (indehiscent) but this shell breaks down in the soil to allow germination.
Organ	A group of tissues which form a structure with a special function. The stem, leaf and root are organs and the female and male parts of the flower are reproductive organs.
Ovary	The swollen base of the carpel which contains the ovules.

Ovule	The small structure in the ovary which contains the female sex cell. If a pollen tube containing the male sex cell reaches the ovule, the flower is fertilised and as it ripens it becomes a seed.
Palisade	The layer of cells beneath the upper epidermis of a leaf. They are tightly packed and contain a high quantity of chlorophyll for photosynthesis.
Pedicel	The stalk of an individual flower.
Peduncle	The stalk of a whole inflorescence.
Perianth	The inner and outer whorls of the flower composed of the corolla (petals) and the calyx (sepals).
Pericarp	The entire wall of the fruit consisting of the exocarp, mesocarp and endocarp.
Petal	A leaf-like structure which forms the inner whorl of a flower. It often attracts the pollinator to the flower by being brightly coloured but it may be green or absent altogether.
Petiole	The stalk which joins a leaf to a node on the stem.
Phloem	Columns of living cells whose horizontal walls are perforated, forming long sieve-like tubes. These transport food substances produced by photosynthesis in the leaves to all other parts according to the time of year and need of the plant.
Pip	The seed of a fruit like apple or orange.
Pith	Soft tissue found in the centre of stems in non-woody dicotyledon plants and usually used for food storage.
Plasmodesmata	Extensions of the cell membrane which join to the adjacent cell wall allowing substances to be passed from cell to cell.
Plumule	Part of the embryo and seedling which becomes the emerging shoot above the cotyledon (seed leaves).
Pod	A long thin fruit developed from one carpel which may contain one or more seeds. The pod splits along a line (dehiscent).
Pollen	Minute structures produced by the anthers in angiosperms and the cones in gymnosperms and which contain the male sex cells. When pollen lands on a stigma, the flower is said to be pollinated and fertilisation normally occurs.

Pome	A fruit where the seeds are enclosed by a core formed by the carpels, surrounded by a large fleshy part which is formed from the receptacle.
Pseudocarp	A type of fruit which contains the seeds, whereby the receptacle has developed into the fruit rather than the ovary.
Radical	The part of the embryo and seedling which develops into the root.
Receptacle	The swollen end of a flower stalk bearing all the parts of the flower.
Rhizome	A stem which grows underground. It can produce buds and roots and therefore enables perennation and vegetative reproduction.
Root	The organ of a plant which grows underground and provides the plant with anchorage, absorbs water and nutrients and can store food.
Root initial	A bulge on a stem or rhizome from where a root will grow.
Root nodule	A small swelling on the root of plants from the Leguminoseae family. It contains bacteria which attract nitrogen from the surrounding air in the soil and fix it into a form that plants can take up via the roots.
Root-cap	A layer of cells at the tip of the root which protects the root as it grows.
Root-hair	Fine hairs which are single-celled and grow out from the root just above the zone of elongation. They absorb water and nutrients.
Runner	A stem which grows along the ground and new plants may grow where the nodes touch the ground. This term is used interchangeably with stolon.
Sapwood	The outer part of the xylem which contains some living cells and transports sap (water and nutrients).
Seed	A fertilised and ripened ovule of an angiosperm or gymnosperm.
Seed leaves	See *cotyledon.*
Sepal	The green leaf-like structure which protects the flower bud and then forms the outer whorl of the flower when it opens.

Shoot Any stem above ground. Often refers to a newly emerging stem.

Simple leaf A leaf which is whole and not divided into leaflets (see appendix).

Spongy mesophyll A layer of loosely packed cells between the palisade and lower epidermis in a leaf where the diffusion of gases takes place.

Spore A small and simple reproductive cell from which new plants are produced in mosses, ferns and fungi.

Stalk A common term either for the main stem of a plant, or for the stem of a leaf (petiole) or flower (pedicel).

Stamen The male reproductive organ of a flower consisting of the anther and the filament.

Stem The main support of a plant which bears buds, flowers and leaves and usually grows above ground. It is used for transporting and storing water and nutrients from the roots to the aerial parts of the plant. Photosynthesis and transpiration also take place here but to a lesser extent than in leaves.

Stigma The swollen tip of the carpel which receives the pollen grains.

Stipule A small leaf-like organ which grows at the base of a petiole or the node on a stem on some plants.

Stolon A stem which grows along the ground. New plants will grow where the nodes touch the ground. This term is used interchangeably with runner.

Stoma (*singular*) **stomata** (*plural*) A breathing pore on stems and leaves but the majority are found on the lower surface of the leaves. The pore is controlled by two guard cells on either side which can open and close the stoma according to water content, light levels and temperature.

Style The stalk of the carpel which joins the stigma to the ovary.

Sucker A stem arising from underground close to the base of the parent plant and usually coming from the rootstock.

Tap root The primary root of a plant with little or no lateral root growth.

Tendril   A modified leaf, stem or petiole which is used to support the plant enabling it to climb up towards the light. When the tendril touches another plant or support, it twists and coils itself around to form a strong grip.

Tepal   When there is no difference between the petals and sepals on a flower they are called tepals.

Testa   The hard outer shell of a seed.

Thorn   A sharp and often hooked spine growing from a stem which is used as defence and for holding onto a supporting plant as it climbs up towards the light.

Tissue   A group of cells which have the same function.

True leaves   The first leaves to appear after the seed leaves or cotyledons.

Tuber   A storage organ which consists of a swollen stem or root underground. It enables perennation and vegetative reproduction.

Vacuole   A space in a cell which is surrounded by membrane. It contains cell sap within which amino acids and waste products are stored.

Vascular bundle   A group of xylem and phloem threads with cambium in between them. These are referred to as the veins.

Vascular system   The xylem and phloem tissues which transport substances from one part of the plant to another.

Vein   A term loosely used to describe the visible lines on a leaf which mark the positions of the vascular systems.

Wood   The organic compound lignin is deposited in the remains of xylem cells in the stem. It makes a hard tissue known as wood for supporting the plant.

Xylem   Columns of cells whose horizontal walls have broken down, forming long tube-like vessels which transport water and nutrients from the roots to all other parts of the plant. Xylem cells die as they mature, making way for new cells to be formed inside the old ones. The dead cells form hard tissue known as wood.

How plants live

Abscission   The natural detachment of leaves, flowers and branches from the plant. It is thought that the process of leaf fall is triggered by the hormone abscissic acid which allows useful chemicals to be reabsorbed into the plant. A thin corky layer then forms at the base of the leaf petiole allowing it to loosen and fall. Leaf abscission means that there is less transpiration throughout the season when the plant is in dormancy, be it winter or summer.

Anemophily   Pollination by wind.

Annual   A plant which completes its lifecycle in one year or growing season.

Apical dominance   Hormones are produced at stem tips which inhibit growth from laterals further down, so that growth is dominated by the apex of the shoot. This explains why pruning off the tip of a stem encourages subsequent growth from laterals still left on that stem.

Apomixis   The production of ripe seed without the sexual fusion of cells. The resulting offspring are genetically identical to the parent.

Asexual reproduction   The production of offspring either by apomixis or by vegetative reproduction.

Auxins   A group of plant hormones involved in many plant processes such as cell growth, secondary thickening and apical dominance. They are produced close to the apex and in young leaves and are then transported to other parts of the plant.

Biennial   A plant which completes its lifecycle within two years or growing seasons.

Bud break   The point in spring when the hormones gibberellin and cytokinin rise to stimulate buds to open and grow.

Callus   A tissue that forms over a wounded part of a plant to seal and protect it.

Carbon   A chemical element that is fundamental to plant life and is found in all organisms.

Carbon cycle   The chemical changes and reactions of carbon and its compounds as it moves from the atmosphere into living organisms, and on their death into the soil and back through all or part of this process again.

Carbon dioxide   A chemical compound made up of carbon and oxygen which is found as a gas in the atmosphere. Carbon dioxide plays a fundamental role in photosynthesis. Plants take in carbon dioxide during the day and use water and the energy of sunlight to convert it into carbohydrates. Oxygen is given off as a by-product. Carbon dioxide is also produced in the process of respiration. This involves the cells using oxygen to release energy from carbohydrates, and water and carbon dioxide are the by-products.

Carnivorous   A plant which traps and ingests insects and other small creatures to obtain nutrients.

Cell division   A cell replication process whereby one cell divides to form two new cells.

Clone   A new plant which is genetically identical to its parent plant because it has been reproduced vegetatively or by apomixis and therefore does not contain genetic material from two parents.

Compatible   Two plants which can breed with each other either by cross-fertilisation or grafting.

Cross-pollination   When pollen is transferred from the anther of one flower to the surface of the stigma of a flower on a separate plant. The two plants may be the same species or closely related.

Cutin   The waxy material that forms the cuticle on leaf and stem surfaces.

Dehiscent   Refers to a fruit which splits open along a line.

Diffusion   The movement of solute molecules from a more concentrated to a less concentrated solution. This is how nutrients are absorbed into the plant cells.

Dioescious   A species which has the male and female flowers on separate plants.

Dormant   A part or all of the plant that is resting, has temporarily stopped growing or is in a period of suspended growth. It is thought to be controlled by hormones. Seeds can remain dormant until factors such as temperature, oxygen and water availability trigger them to germinate. Similarly, the entire plant can be dormant at some point in the year due to climate change.

Entomophily   Pollination by insects.

Ephemeral   Describes a plant which completes its lifecycle within weeks. This usually gives rise to many generations within one year or growing season.

Etiolation   When there is insufficient light for a plant it produces rapid growth with unusually extended internodes and often pale leaves as it tries to reach more light in order to produce chlorophyll. The plant is often referred to as 'leggy' or 'drawn'.

Fertile   Capable of producing seeds which will germinate. A plant is said to be fertile if it produces ripe pollen, has receptive female reproductive organs or has fruit which contains seed.

Fertilisation   The fusion of the male and female sex cells (contained within the pollen grain and ovule) to form an embryo. This is achieved after the pollen grain has landed on the stigma, grown a tube down to the ovule and entered it.

Genetically modified organism (GMO)   Any living organism, including plants, which has had its genetic material deliberately altered in the breeding process.

Genetics   The study of the inherited characteristics of a plant.

Germination   The period of growth from a seed to a seedling. It starts with a seed taking in water and ends with the production of the first true leaves.

Hermaphrodite   Flowers which contain both the female and male reproductive organs (the style, stigma and ovary and the filament and anther respectively).

Hormones   Different chemical messengers that determine and control growth and development of the plant.

Hybridisation The act of cross-fertilising two species or genera to produce a new cultivar. This may be done artificially by growers or occur naturally in the wild.

Hydrogen A chemical element which is found as a trace gas in the atmosphere and is combined with oxygen to form water. It is fundamental to plant life.

Incompatible Two plants which cannot breed with each other.

Indehiscent Refers to a fruit which does not split open along a line.

Inorganic Compounds which do not contain carbon.

Lifecycle The life of a plant from seed germination to root and shoot development, then flower production, pollination, fertilisation and seed dispersal through to the death of the plant.

Meiosis A cell replication process in the sex organs (anther and ovary) which produces pollen and ovules which individually have half the chromosomes of the parent cell. If fertilisation occurs between the pollen and ovules, the resulting embryo will have the full set of chromosomes, half from each parent cell.

Mitosis A cell replication process in the meristem which produces plant growth. The nucleus of one cell divides, the chromosomes replicate themselves over several phases and an identical new cell is formed.

Monocarpic Describes a plant which dies after setting seed. Usually applies to plants which live for several years before flowering, setting seed and then dying.

Monoecious Species which have separate male and female flowers but on the same plant.

Organic Compounds which contain carbon.

Ornithophily Pollination by birds.

Osmosis The movement of water molecules from a weak solution to a stronger solution through a semi-permeable membrane. When water is readily available in the soil, it flows into the plant and will pass from one cell to another until the balance

> **TOP TIP**
>
> **To help pollinate a plant**
> Use a small paintbrush to brush the pollen from one flower onto the stigma of another.

of solution is met. This means that water will travel through a plant to areas where it is most needed.

Oxygen   A chemical element which exists as a gas in the atmosphere. It is fundamental to plant life as it is utilised in respiration. It also combines with hydrogen to form water.

Parthenocarpy The production of fruit without seeds when fertilisation has not occurred.

Perennation The occurrence of plants surviving from season to season. Usually applies to non-woody plants, many of which die down during winter with the roots being unaffected by frost damage.

Perennial   A plant whose lifecycle covers more than two years and does not die after flowering.

Photoperiod   The number of hours of daylight that a plant needs in order for it to flower.

Photosynthesis The chemical process whereby green plants produce carbohydrates, such as starch and glucose, from carbon dioxide and water. The energy for this process is obtained by the chlorophyll absorbing sunlight. Oxygen is given off as a by-product.

Plasmolysis   When water passes out of a cell into a stronger solution by osmosis. This causes the vacuole and the protoplasm to shrink away from the cell wall and damages the plasmodesmata. This can happen if the soil is over-fertilised.

Pollination   When pollen is carried from the anther to the surface of the stigma in angiosperms and from the male cone to the female cone in gymnosperms.

Protoandrous Flowers in which the male organs become mature and produce pollen before the female organs are functional, in order to prevent self pollination.

Protogynous   Flowers in which the female organs become mature and functional before the male organs, in order to prevent self pollination.

Respiration   A series of chemical processes in cells which release energy from carbohydrates to form carbon dioxide and water. Aerobic respiration involves oxygen and there is a complete breakdown of carbohydrates, whereas anaerobic respiration occurs when the cells do not use oxygen and there is only a partial breakdown of carbohydrates.

Secondary thickening The thickening of a stem or root due to cell division in the cambium.

Seed dispersal The distribution of seed in different directions by a number of means including using animals, wind and water. Some plants have mechanical devices of their own such as seedpods splitting violently or fruits which twist and can squirt the seeds a fair distance.

Self-pollination Pollination when pollen is transferred from the anther to the surface of the stigma in the same flower or to another flower on the same plant.

Sexual reproduction The process which involves the fusion of two cells from two individual parents to produce offspring. The offspring receives genetic material from both parents.

Sterile Plants which cannot produce fruit, seeds or spores and therefore offspring. Many hybrid plants are sterile.

Translocation The movement of substances from one part of the plant to another via the xylem and phloem.

Transpiration The loss of water vapour from a plant through the stomata in the leaves which induces the movement of water upwards through the plant.

Tropism The direction of growth of a plant organ in response to external stimuli. Phototropism is where the organ grows towards or away from light. Geotropism is upward or downward growth in response to gravity. Hydrotropism is the direction of growth controlled by water and thigmotropism is the curving of a plant organ when it touches an object.

Turgid The state of a cell when it is full to capacity with water and can absorb no more. It is the balance between osmosis and the elasticity of the cell wall.

Vegetative reproduction The production of offspring from any part of the parent plant other than the male and female sexual organs. The offspring are genetically identical to the parent.

Viability   The capability of a seed to survive in a dormant state whilst retaining the ability to germinate when conditions are right. Some seeds may only be viable until the next growing season whereas others may have viability for years.

Wilt   Droop of the plant leaves and stems caused by a lack of water in the cells. This could be due to insufficient water in the soil, or to transpiration being greater than the uptake of water by the roots.

Producing plants

Growing media

Bark   An organic material made from chipped and sterilised bark from trees. It is mixed with other materials to provide a potting compost with good aeration and drainage and contains virtually no nutrients. It can be partly composted and is relatively expensive.

Coir   A by-product of the coconut industry. It is the brown fibre found outside the coconut shell and is washed off in the de-husking process. It can be used as a soil conditioner or finely shredded to provide a compost ingredient. It has recently become accepted as a good alternative to peat-based composts in propagation and potting plants. It provides good structure to a compost and is moisture-retentive.

Compost   Loosely describes any materials which have been mixed to produce a specialised growing medium either for seeds to germinate, cuttings to root or plants to grow. Compost is used instead of soil, which gives poor results in containers. The base ingredient in any compost is either loam, peat or coir. Sand, grit, perlite, vermiculite and organic matter may be added to varying degrees depending on the type of compost. In this sense, the term is used interchangeably with growing medium. See also *garden compost*.

Cuttings compost   A growing medium which is used to root cuttings. It is usually loam, peat or coir-based with silver sand and vermiculite. Cuttings compost should preferably be low in nutrients and moisture-retentive with good drainage.

> **TOP TIP**
>
> **Sterilised sand**
> Always use horticultural sand which has been sterilised. Never use builder's sand as it tends to clog and compact the compost.

60

Ericaceous compost A growing medium with the base ingredient of loam with added sulphur, or peat or composted pine bark, the last two being naturally acidic. It is used for calcifuge plants which prefer acid soils, including species from the Ericaceous family. Fertilisers that are incorporated into the compost do not contain any forms of calcium.

Garden compost/compost The humus-rich soil which is the result of composting and is brown and crumbly and should have a soil-like aroma. This compost is mixed with other materials to form a growing medium. It is moisture-retentive, provides aeration and also contains nutrients so is a useful ingredient for improving the structure and fertility of a growing medium.

General-purpose compost Either a loam-based but more usually a peat or coir-based compost which is much used for a wide range of growing purposes. It can be used for raising seeds, rooting cuttings or for crop or ornamental planting. The nutrients or fertilisers that it contains will normally only last for one to two months. It is relatively cheap and widely available.

Grit Coarse sand mixed with irregular particles of stone which are roughly between 2mm and 10mm in diameter. It does not bind strongly to water or nutrients and is used to improve aeration and drainage in potting composts. It is also frequently used like a mulch or top dressing on the surface of seed compost to reduce damping off diseases and for ornamental purposes. Grit has no nutrient value.

Growbag A plastic bag, usually containing a peat-based or loam-based compost, into which slits or holes are made and young plants are planted into the compost through these holes. It is commonly used for planting annual vegetables, especially tomatoes.

Growing medium Any material, organic or inorganic, in which seeds, cuttings or plants can be grown in a container. It can be a single material or a mix of materials to produce seed composts, cuttings composts and potting composts. A growing medium should, to a greater or lesser extent, support the plant root system, provide aeration, and balance moisture retention with drainage.

Some will also provide nutrients. The term is used interchangeably with compost.

Hydroponics A method of growing plants without compost as the growing media but with water and nutrients only. This solution is constantly flowing and therefore being replaced with fresh solution. The plants are tied into a support because the roots do not provide any anchorage. The plants also form relatively small roots and root systems because they do not have to search for water and nutrients.

John Innes compost A loam-based compost, the recipe for which was produced by the John Innes Institute (JI) in the 1930's. JI Seed & Cutting Compost is made from two parts loam, one part peat to one part sand or grit plus lime and a phosphorus fertiliser. JI Potting Compost No 1, No 2 and No 3 are made from seven parts loam, three parts peat and two parts sand or grit plus lime and nitrogen, phosphorus and potassium fertilisers. No 3 has three times more fertiliser than No 1.

Leaf mould Leaves which have decomposed into a crumbly compost. This is usually mixed with other materials to make a potting compost. It is moisture-retentive, provides aeration and also contains nutrients so is a useful ingredient for improving the structure and fertility of a growing medium.

Loam A type of soil which contains a mixture of sand, silt and clay particles. A good loam will contain around 40% sand, 30% silt and 30% clay as well as a small amount of organic matter. It can occur naturally, or be made commercially or be home-made. Loam is often used as a base to which other ingredients are added to make composts for more specialised purposes. Commercial loam usually contains enough nutrients for the average plant for about one month. Alternatives to loam are now being found due to the difficulty of obtaining good loam.

> **TOP TIP**
>
> **Keep your empty compost bags**
> Use them instead of bin bags for collecting up leaves and weeds or going down the dump!

Loam-based compost A compost which has loam as its main ingredient.

Moss A primitive plant which produces spores instead of seeds and depends on water for reproduction. Sphagnum moss is most commonly harvested and can be mixed with other materials to provide a compost with good moisture retention and structure. It is sometimes used alone or packed around a pole to provide a moist support for plants with adventitious roots.

Peat A growing medium derived from a soil with a high quantity of undecomposed organic matter which has become compressed under its own weight. There are generally two types of peat, sphagnum or sedge. Both have a fibrous, spongy texture, are moisture-retentive but can dry out quickly, contain little or no available nutrients and, visibly, are almost black in colour. Alternatives to peat are now being found and used due to the destruction of rare habitats during the harvesting of the peat.

Peat block/peat pellet Peat which has been shredded, sieved, compressed into a block and punctured with holes for inserting cuttings or seedlings. It is mainly used in nurseries where plants are mass propagated.

Peat pot A container made out of peat in which plants are grown. The benefit is that the plant and the pot can be planted out or potted on reducing root disturbance. The pot does break down allowing the roots to extend outwards.

Peat-based compost A compost which has peat as its main ingredient.

Perlag Clay aggregates which have been heated and processed into the form of spherical balls about 10mm in diameter. They are inert, sterile and lightweight and are mixed with other materials to provide potting composts with aeration and drainage as well as moisture retention. They can also be used as crocks or on benches in greenhouses underneath pots in the same way as capillary matting.

Perlite An inorganic material derived from volcanic rock which is crushed and heated rapidly. It expands to form a lightweight, white granule which does not break down in composts. It is sterile with a neutral pH and does not contain any nutrients. It is mixed with other materials primarily to make potting composts which are well-drained and aerated.

Potting compost A growing medium which is used to pot on seedlings, rooted cuttings and established plants. It is usually loam, peat or coir-based with sand, perlite or grit added depending upon the purpose. It may also contain additional fertilisers for all-round plant growth and development.

Rock wool A growing medium manufactured from granite, limestone and coke which are processed into fibres. These are consolidated by a binding and wetting agent to produce blocks which can be cut to size and used for the insertion of cuttings and seedlings. These blocks are reusable. Alternatively, it is used as a wool to improve the structure of potting composts. It is sterile and virtually nutrient-free.

Sand Soil particles which are between 0.02mm and 2mm in diameter. They are unweathered pieces of rock and do not bind strongly to water or nutrients. Silver sand and sharp sand, which are produced from graded and sterilised fine and coarse sand, are used as growing media when mixed with other materials.

Sedge peat Peat which is cut from bogs on which sedges, reeds, grasses and heathers grow. It is darker, more decomposed and less moisture-retentive than sphagnum peat.

Seed compost A growing medium which is used to germinate seeds. It is usually loam, peat or coir-based with sand and perlite. Seed compost should preferably be low in nutrients with good aeration and drainage.

Sharp sand Large particles of sand between 0.2mm and 2mm in diameter which have been sterilised. It is mixed with other materials to make potting composts with good aeration and drainage and contains no nutrients.

Silver sand Small particles of sand between 0.02mm and 0.2mm in diameter which have been sterilised. It is mixed with other materials to provide a specialist potting compost for plants which require no added nutrients, well-drained conditions and have roots which can tolerate baking if the compost gets hot and dry. It is also used as an ingredient in a seed or cuttings compost.

Sphagnum peat Peat which is cut from bogs on which sphagnum mosses grow. It is lighter in colour, less decomposed and more moisture-retentive than sedge peat.

Sterilise Removing micro-organisms from the growing media by steam or heat treatment. This kills pests, diseases and weed seeds.

Topsoil Derived from the top layer of soil which contains the plant roots, organic matter, micro-organisms and nutrients. Topsoil should have a good structure and be dark in colour. Commercial topsoil is expensive and is really only used for structures such as raised beds or in gardens with a shallow topsoil. In this case, the additional topsoil should be the same texture and pH as the existing soil.

Vermiculite An inorganic material derived from an aluminium-iron-magnesium silicate. It is heated so that steam pressure causes it to separate in layers to produce lightweight flakes which contain minute air pockets. It is sterile, improves drainage and aeration and is able to absorb water and nutrients and give them up easily to the plant. It is mixed with other materials primarily to make seed and cutting composts.

Propagation and growing on

Across the grain Describes the way a cut is made through a stem whether it is woody or green. It is made from one side of the stem through taking the shortest distance.

Air layering A form of vegetative propagation usually used on shrubs and houseplants which have outgrown their allotted space and do not produce suitable stems close enough to the ground for conventional layering. A sturdy stem from the previous year's growth is selected in the spring but not detached from the parent plant. The leaves and side shoots are removed from a section of about 30cm long. A cut is made into the stem and the knife is drawn towards the stem tip, with the grain, for about 2.5cm without removing any wood. The cut is packed with moist moss to hold it open, then the entire stem around the wound is wrapped in damp moss and sealed in a plastic bag or similar. If the moss is kept moist, most species will root by autumn although some may take up to two years.

Bark graft See *rind graft.*

Basal cutting A form of vegetative propagation which is used less often than other forms of cuttings, but is good for plants which do not produce suitable vegetative growth for stem cuttings. The cuttings are taken in early spring, just as the first flush of growth has started to unfurl at the crown of the root ball. This growth is cut with a small amount of the hard older wood at its base and the lowest leaves are trimmed away. It is sometimes possible to find these new stems with a few roots attached. The cuttings should root in about one to two months.

Base heat/bottom heat Heat that is artificially supplied to the base of pots. The heating system is usually enclosed in the bench, floor or material on which they stand. Base heat encourages and promotes rooting so is often used under pots of cuttings and young plants. Similarly, base heat is supplied beneath pots of seeds because most seeds require a minimum temperature in order to germinate.

Bottom working Grafting techniques where the scion is attached to the rootstock close to the level of the ground.

Broadcast sowing A method of sowing seed by scattering it over the soil or compost surface rather than placing it in deliberate positions.

Budding/bud grafting A type of grafting where a bud from the scion is grafted to the stem of the rootstock. This produces trees and shrubs with a strong graft union and includes the techniques of chip budding and T-budding.

Callus A tissue that forms over a wounded part of a plant to seal and protect it. A callus forms at the base of cuttings and the roots will develop from this area.

Chip budding A grafting technique which is used to propagate mainly fruit trees and roses from mid to late summer by attaching a bud from the scion material to the stem of the rootstock. The bud is cut away from the scion with about 2cm of wood above and below it and includes about 5mm of cambium behind it. The base of this chip needs to be cut to make it wedge-shaped. The smooth stem of the rootstock needs to be cut in a concave shape corresponding to the bud chip. The chip is wedged into the rootstock cut and sealed with plastic or a rubber budding tie. When a callus forms around the bud, the union is made and the plastic can be removed and the bud should grow.

Chipping A form of vegetative propagation for some bulbs that do not readily divide or set seed. The bulb tip and roots are cut away then the bulb is cut in half from the tip to the base to form two chips. Each chip is then sliced in the same way and repeated to provide eight to sixteen chips, depending on the size of the bulb, each with a segment of the basal plate. These can then be soaked in a fungicide and then sealed in a bag of moist vermiculite and left in a dark warm place for around three months. Young bulblets should form between the leaf scales of each chip and these can be removed and potted up or the entire chip can be planted.

Chitted seed   Seed which is germinated before it is sown. The seed is spread thinly on moist absorbent paper and placed in a plastic box with a lid in a warm place. The seed should germinate in a few days and can then be carefully sown. The purpose of this method is to check the viability of the seed or to allow germination when the temperature is too low outside.

Chitting   Germinating seed before it is sown. The term is more widely used to describe the process of sprouting potatoes before planting them. This is done by placing them in a cool, but frost-free, and light place for around six to eight weeks prior to planting. New shoots will sprout from the eyes and these will produce the top growth of the potatoes.

Cloche   A mobile protective structure, traditionally a glass bell, which is placed over a plant. It is mainly used to raise early crops or to give frost protection to tender perennials. It can also be used to keep plants dry in the winter. Glass is still the preferred material, although clear polythene is often used.

Clone   A new plant which is genetically identical to its parent plant because it has been reproduced vegetatively or by apomixis and therefore does not contain genetic material from two parents.

Closed case   A mini-greenhouse within a greenhouse. It is mainly used for pots of seeds which require a warmer temperature to germinate, and normally consists of a frame with a glass or plastic lid. The lid can be raised to improve ventilation or to remove any build-up of condensation. It can also be used for plants which require a higher humidity than the rest of the greenhouse, for example, cuttings from tropical plants or ferns.

Crown graft   See *rind graft.*

Cutting   A form of vegetative propagation by removing a part of the plant, usually the stem, leaf or root, and inserting it into a growing medium to allow root formation and subsequent development of a new plant. A cutting will produce a clone and is ideal for plants which are difficult to divide or do not come true from seed.

Division A form of vegetative propagation which simply involves splitting the parent plant into two or more sections. Each section must have roots and top growth or the potential for this growth if it is dormant. It is best to divide plants in spring before new growth starts but it can also be done in autumn for spring-flowering plants. Plants which spread from a central crown are perfect for division and the old centre is usually discarded with new plants being divided from the vigorous growth around the edges. This technique is also essential to keep perennial plants healthy with optimum flowering. Bulbs can also be divided as they produce offsets which can be easily but gently pulled away from the mother bulb during dormancy.

Double worked A grafting technique whereby a rootstock is grafted to an intermediary scion which is then grafted to a flowering and fruiting scion. This is used with fruit trees such as pears when the rootstock and fruiting scion are incompatible or to obtain another beneficial characteristic not provided by the rootstock.

Dwarf/dwarfing Describes a rootstock species which when grafted to the scion species will give the resulting plant a smaller than normal height. This is useful for fruit trees for smaller gardens and for ease of harvesting.

Early sowings Seed sown earlier than is recommended by giving it some kind of protection in order to allow it to germinate and grow on. Early sowings can be made in the greenhouse before being moved outside or under cloches in situ. This technique gives these plants a head start and also extends the harvesting season for that crop.

Fleecy film/floating fleece Lightweight fleece which is placed over seeds, young seedlings or a crop to act as frost, wind and pest protection whilst allowing water and light to pass through. The fleece can be weighted down or pegged at the sides and the plants lift the fleece as they grow.

Fluid sowing/fluid drilling A method of sowing seed in a gel or paste into drills via a plastic bag with the corner cut off. This is a useful technique for very fine seed, or for chitted seed so as not to damage the roots.

Frame-working Grafting which is done to change the cultivar of a tree, particularly fruit trees. The main framework of the tree is kept but the laterals are pruned back. The scion of the new cultivar is then grafted on to these areas.

Germination The period of growth from a seed to a seedling. It starts with a seed taking in water and ends with the production of the first true leaves.

Grading Describes the process of choosing similarly-sized seedlings whilst pricking out.

Graft union See *union*.

Grafting A propagating technique popular with woody plants in open ground. Grafting involves many techniques of artificially joining a piece of vegetative material from one plant (scion) to the rootstock of another. The scion and rootstock are usually the same species but may be a different cultivar. The cambium of the scion and rootstock join together and grow to form a new plant with characteristics from both parents. Grafting can be used to produce plants with a special form or habit, to produce plants which are difficult to propagate by conventional methods or do not come true from seed, to change or add a cultivar to an existing tree, to repair a damaged tree or shrub and/or to produce trees and shrubs which reach maturity in a shorter space of time than by seed or cuttings. Additional to this is to obtain the characteristics of a particular rootstock, be it vigour, pest and disease resistance, tolerance to a soil type and/or earlier or increased flowering and fruiting. Grafting techniques include budding, side-veneer grafting, whip and tongue grafting and rind grafting.

Grow on The period of growing and tending a seedling once it has been pricked out, or a plant once it has been potted on.

Harden off The process of gradually moving young plants from the environmental conditions in which they were propagated to cooler conditions in preparation for planting them outside permanently. For example, from a mist bench to a regular bench in the greenhouse then to a cold frame, with a little more ventilation each day before planting out. Mature plants which have been growing in a greenhouse must also be hardened off before being planted outside. The cooler conditions allow the plants to harden their stems and become generally more sturdy, whilst still being afforded some protection from cold weather to ensure their survival. This gentle acclimatisation reduces shock to the plant and allows the grower greater control over the plant in its young stage of growth.

Hardwood cutting A stem cutting taken in autumn after leaf fall, winter or early spring before bud break. The cutting should be taken from vigorous, current season's wood when plant growth has stopped, the tissues have ripened and the cutting is therefore dormant. The cutting is inserted in open ground so less environmental control is required. This technique is used for propagating mainly deciduous trees and shrubs but does take longer than with softwood cuttings.

Heel The base of a stem cutting which has been pulled gently away from the main stem of the parent plant. The heel is the piece of older wood from the main stem and looks like a heel or foot.

Heel cutting A semi-ripe cutting which is taken with a heel at its base to help reduce rot. The heel also provides an increased area from which roots can develop.

In situ In the permanent growing position. Seeds can be sown in situ as opposed to in a greenhouse, seed bed or nursery bed.

Internodal cuttings A stem cutting where the base cut is made halfway between two nodes on the stem. This is most common in propagating Clematis and Fuschia species.

Interstock/interstem The intermediary scion which is used in a double worked graft.

Juvenile wood A stem which is from this season's growth. It is pliable and full of auxins and so is a more suitable material for cuttings than older wood.

Layering A form of vegetative propagation, common with woody plants or those which do not root very easily from cuttings. A stem which is low on the plant is bent down to the ground and weighted, secured or buried so that it is in full contact with the ground. The part that is in contact is wounded and roots should develop from here. Subsequently a new plant is produced which can be cut away from the parent. The benefit of this method of propagation is that the layered stem is still attached to the stock plant so that it continues to receive food until it is severed. Layering is best carried out in the spring and should root by the autumn, but is left in place until the following spring.

Leaf cutting A form of vegetative propagation which uses a part or all of a leaf to produce a new plant. This includes leaf-bud, leaf-lamina and leaf-petiole cuttings and the best time for these is spring or when the plant is in active growth.

Leaf-bud cutting A cutting which uses a single leaf and its petiole attached to a section of the stem from which it was taken, with a bud in the axil. The stem is cut just above the bud and about 2.5cm below the leaf petiole. The leaf-bud cutting is then treated as a semi-ripe cutting. This method is used to propagate plants which have buds in the leaf axils and cuttings are taken in late summer to early autumn. The benefit is that a number of cuttings can be taken from one stem.

Leaf-lamina cutting A cutting which uses an entire leaf or portion of a leaf but not the petiole. The leaf can be laid flat onto the growing media, right side up, and pinned down to ensure contact. Large entire leaves can be scored with a sharp knife across the raised veins to produce new plants at each wound. Alternatively large leaves can be cut into squares as long as each section contains a strong vein at the centre. The leaf can also be cut in half or into sections with the cut edge being inserted into the growing media. Leaf-lamina cuttings usually take around six weeks to root and form plantlets.

Leaf-petiole cutting A cutting which uses a single leaf and its petiole to produce a new plant. The petiole can be cut to about 2.5cm long and then fully inserted into the growing media so that the base of the leaf is just touching the compost. The cutting should root within a month and produce plantlets at the base of the leaf within two months.

Mallet cutting A stem cutting which consists of a side shoot joined to a small section of main stem which is woody and possibly from the previous season's growth. The main stem is cut just above the side shoot and again about 2cm below the side shoot to produce the cutting. This is a useful technique with species that are prone to rotting.

Misting The regular and frequent delivery of a fine spray of water to the foliage of a plant, and especially to cuttings. Misting increases humidity on and around the leaves so reduces transpiration. This is vitally important for the survival and development of cuttings because they continue to transpire after they have been severed from the growing plant, yet have no roots to take up and replace the lost water. This rapidly leads to wilting and the death of the cutting if misting does not take place.

Multiple seeding/sowing To sow a number of seeds in one position. The intention is to thin out the weaker seedlings once they have germinated or to leave the seedlings to grow into a clump where they can push for space.

Nodal cutting A stem cutting where the base cut is made just below a node on the stem and the lowest leaves are removed. This is the most common method with stem cuttings.

Nurse grafting Grafting techniques which are used to repair damaged branches, usually at the top of the trunk or in the canopy of the rootstock.

Nursery bed An area of ground which is set aside specifically for raising seedlings and young plants before they are planted out in their permanent positions. The idea is that they need less space at this stage in their life so can be grown closer together and do not require thinning until they are planted out so it is an efficient use of space in the garden.

Open ground Refers to plants which are growing outside as opposed to container-grown plants.

Pollinator grafting Grafting techniques where a scion from a cultivar, which is particularly free-flowering and produces abundant virile pollen, is grafted to another cultivar of tree within the same genus, so that pollination is increased in the main cultivar. This is often used on crab apples and in orchards.

Pot on To take a plant out of one pot and replant it into a larger container with fresh compost. This is done frequently in the early stages after germination, and then preferably every spring depending on the rate of growth. The new pot should be no larger than one or two sizes bigger than the previous pot.

Pot-bound A potted plant whose roots have filled the entire pot and may be growing out from the holes in the bottom. The roots may also be growing around themselves which can lead to the death of the plant if it is not potted on. Time should be taken to tease the roots out from this state before potting on or planting. Some plants flower better when they are pot-bound but they do need to be fed.

Pre-treated seed Seed which can be obtained which has already been released from dormancy by scarification or stratification and is therefore ready to germinate under the right conditions. It can also refer to seed which has been soaked in fungicide and must be handled with care. This may also be referred to as primed seed.

Prick out Transferring seedlings into larger containers after they have germinated and before they become too crowded. This is usually done once the seedlings have their first set of true leaves, or when they are large enough to handle by the seed leaves.

Primed seed See *pre-treated seed*.

Propagation Producing a new plant or plants by sowing seed or by a number of vegetative methods including cuttings, division, grafting and layering.

Propagator A mini-greenhouse comprising of at least a tray base and clear lid into which pots of seeds or cuttings are placed. It creates a warm and humid micro-climate within a greenhouse or on the windowsill. Some propagators come with small ventilation holes and electric heating systems at their base.

Provenance The place of origin of a plant. This usually refers to where the seed, cutting or whole plant was collected in the wild.

Repotting The process of removing a plant from the container in which it has been growing and planting it into a larger container with fresh growing media. This is usually done each spring before the plant becomes pot-bound. The plant should be potted into pots no larger than one or two sizes bigger.

Rind graft/bark graft/crown graft A grafting technique which is employed when the rootstock is noticeably larger in diameter than the scion. This may be because the framework of the rootstock tree has been pollarded prior to grafting. A vertical cut is made into the bark about 2.5cm long from the top of the rootstock branch. The bark is peeled back to reveal the cambium. The scion should be prepared with three buds on it and a tapering base about 2.5cm long. The scion base is inserted into the bark slit so that both cambium layers meet. The bark is closed around the scion and the graft is sealed with twine and wax or tape. It is usual to graft two or three scions in this manner around the circumference of each rootstock branch, the strongest of these can then be selected once the unions have formed. Rind grafting is carried out in spring.

Ripe Describes a seed which is fully developed and will drop naturally from the parent plant or can be collected by the gardener. Ripe seed is usually hard and dark in colour and can be sown immediately or at the beginning of the following growing season. Some seed may be ripe but in a state of dormancy. The term also describes stems of woody plants when they have turned brown and are woody towards the end of the growing season, as opposed to green and soft during the growing season.

Root cutting A method of vegetative propagation which simply utilises the ability of the plant to regenerate itself from a small part of root. It is ideal for plants with thick fleshy roots or rhizomes, or for those which do not divide easily or propagate well from other types of cuttings. Root cuttings are taken during the dormant period of the plant by cutting pencil-thick roots into

5cm to 7.5cm long sections with a sloping cut at the base and a flat cut at the top. They are then inserted vertically into the compost, ensuring that they are the correct way up (the same way as when attached to the stock plant) or they will not root. Rhizomes can be diced into sections which have both root initials and at least one growing point.

Rootball   The mass of roots and soil bound together on a plant.

Rooting hormone/rooting powder/root promoter A synthetic hormone in powdered or liquid form into which the base cuts of cuttings are dipped to aid the formation of roots.

Rootstock   A plant which is used for its root system to which a scion is grafted to produce a grafted tree or shrub. The rootstock may provide a short stem or the entire trunk with or without a part of the branch framework. The rootstock and scion are usually the same species but may be different cultivars.

Scarification   Enabling a seed to germinate by mechanically breaking down the seed coat to allow it to take in moisture. In the seed's natural environment this may take many years but gardeners can emulate this by scoring, scraping or roughening up the hard seed coat.

Scion   The bud or stem of a plant which is grafted on to the rootstock of another. The scion and rootstock are usually the same species but may be different cultivars.

Seed   A fertilised and ripened ovule of a plant. With the correct growing medium, temperature and moisture level the seed will germinate if it is viable.

Seed leaves   The first leaves of a plant which have stored food for the seed and become the initial photosynthetic organs for the germinated seedling. Also known as the cotyledons.

Seedbed   An area of ground which is set aside specifically for raising seedlings. The seeds are sown closer than the recommended spacings, before being transplanted to their permanent positions.

> **TOP TIP**
>
> **Umbellifereae, Ranculaceae and Primulaceae families**
> Sow the seeds as soon as they are ripe. They tend to lose viability if they are stored until spring.

This is an economic way of using the ground and ideally cuts down on the amount of discarded seedlings due to thinning.

Seedling   A germinated seed with a root and seed leaves. There is some interpretation as to when a seedling becomes a plant, for example, when it has its first true leaves or when it has been pricked out.

Semi-ripe cutting   A stem cutting taken from mid-summer to late autumn from plants that are actively in growth. The cutting should be taken from current season's growth that has started to go brown and ripen and is less pliable than a softwood cutting. The cutting is inserted into a specialist growing medium and usually rooted under glass, so more environmental control is required than for hardwood cuttings. This technique is used for propagating shrubs which have a slow development or late period of growth in the year. They root quickly in around one to two months.

Side grafting   Any method of grafting where the scion is inserted into the side of the rootstock. When the graft union has formed, the rootstock is cut away just above the union.

Side-veneer graft   The most common grafting technique used for propagating trees. It can also be used with both evergreen and deciduous shrubs and is usually done just before bud break in mid to late winter. The rootstock should be up to three years old with a pencil-thick stem. A notch is made in the rootstock, firstly by making a downward cut at an angle of 45°, about 2.5cm above the base of the stem. Then another cut is made 2.5cm above this one which slices down to meet it and the section is removed. The pencil thick scion, about 20cm long, is prepared by making a 2.5cm sloping cut with a wedge at the base. The scion is then inserted into the notch of the rootstock and the graft is secured with tape. Once the graft has taken the rootstock is cut back above the union.

Softwood cutting   A stem cutting taken in spring to early summer from plants that are actively in growth. The cutting should be taken from the first flush of new growth which is green, pliable and full of auxins. The cutting is inserted into a specialist growing medium and usually rooted under glass so more environmental control is required than for hardwood cuttings. This technique is used for propagating shrubs and herbaceous perennials which have an early development and period of growth in the year. They root quickly in around two weeks to two months.

Sow   The action of placing or scattering seeds onto or into soil or a growing medium for them to germinate. Seeds which are sown should be lightly covered with a thin layer of soil, compost or grit and then watered.

Sow thinly   To sow seed in a continuous line in a drill or over the entire surface of soil rather than place deliberately in a set position. The important factor is that they have enough space to germinate without too much competition but can be thinned to the correct spacing once they are seedlings. This usually applies to smaller seed such as those from the Umbellifereae family.

Spacing   The ideal distance between seeds or plants to allow them enough room to germinate or the plants to fully develop to their optimum size. The term is used when sowing seed and planting out, and also for the distance between rows.

Standing ground   Usually an outdoor area, although it may be protected, where potted plants are kept prior to being planted out. The plants have usually been propagated, potted on and hardened off but may still need watering and feeding.

Station sow   To sow seed in deliberate set positions along a drill or bed. Individual seeds or a group of seeds may be placed at set distances apart. This usually applies to larger seeds such as legumes.

Stem cutting   Any type of cutting which is taken from a stem when the plant is in a period of strong growth. The benefit of stem cutting is that a number of cuttings can be taken from one stem.

Stem tip cutting   A type of softwood cutting which can be taken from almost any perennial plant from early spring to summer when the plant is in a period of strong growth. The tips of healthy stems are used, ensuring that they are not flowering. Each cutting should be about 5cm to 7.5cm long with a horizontal cut below a node. The bottom third of leaves is trimmed before inserting into compost.

Sterilisation The killing of micro-organisms and weed seeds from the growing media by steam or heat treatment. Pots, tools and other equipment are also sterilised, usually with a bleach solution or methylated spirit to maintain good hygiene during propagation and avoid spreading diseases.

Stock plant The plant from which cuttings are taken to make new plants. It is usually well-established and should produce healthy vigorous growth. The plant may be pruned more than usual to produce more vegetative growth rather than flowers. All cuttings taken from the stock plant will produce plants which are identical.

Stratification The process of breaking a seed from its dormancy by exposing it to low temperatures around freezing whilst it is moist. Temperatures of around 0.5°C to 5°C are usually chilly enough to break dormancy without freezing the seed. This can be done by mixing seed with moist sand and storing it in the fridge for a period, or by sowing the seed in autumn and allowing it to germinate in pots outside in areas with cold winters.

Successional sowing Sowing seeds of the same crop repeatedly through the season. This ensures a constant supply of that crop and hopefully avoids gluts. It also prevents the whole crop being wiped out by adverse weather conditions or pests.

T-budding A grafting technique which is used mainly to propagate fruit trees and roses from mid to late summer by inserting a bud from the scion material into the stem of the rootstock. The bud is cut away from the scion with about 2cm of wood above and below it and includes about 5mm of cambium behind it. The smooth bark of the rootstock needs scoring like the letter T so that the bark can be peeled back to reveal the cambium. The bud chip is inserted in and under the bark of the rootstock. This is then sealed with plastic or a rubber budding tie. When a callus forms around the bud, the union is made and the plastic can be removed and the bud should grow.

Thinning   The process of selectively weeding out excess seedlings so that the remainder can develop to their optimum size. This is normally done when more than enough seeds have been sown. The weak or damaged seedlings are preferably taken out, ensuring the ones that are left are at the ideal spacing for growth.

Top dressing The removal of the top layer of compost in a pot and replacement with fresh compost. This gets rid of any moss, moulds and weeds, for example, and is normally done in autumn when the plant is to stay in the pot rather than be planted out.

Top working   Grafting where the scion is attached to the rootstock at the top of the trunk or onto pollarded branches. Top working is done, for example, to change the cultivar of a tree, particularly fruit trees.

Transplant   To move a plant from one growing position to another. The term can also apply to the actual plant that is being moved.

True leaves   The first leaves to appear after the seed leaves or cotyledons.

Under glass   Refers to the propagation and growing of plants in a greenhouse or other protected structure. The term is often used to differentiate between seeds that are germinated in a greenhouse rather than in open ground. Seeds that are sown under glass usually produce earlier crops, and tender plants are raised under glass for protection or to give an extended growing season.

Union/graft union The point where a scion and rootstock joins. As a grafted tree gets older the union may appear as a swollen part of the trunk or branch.

Vegetative   Any part of the plant not involved in sexual reproduction.

Vegetative propagation The production of new plants by means other than by seed. This includes cuttings, division and layering, which produce clones, and grafting.

Viable seed   Seed which has the ability to germinate.

Whip and tongue graft A common grafting technique carried out in late winter or early spring as buds are breaking on the rootstock. The scion material should have been cut from the parent plant in mid-winter when it is dormant and stored in a cool and dry place. To make the graft, the rootstock stem is cut back with a sloping cut about 3.5cm long and about 20cm from the base. A downward slit of 1cm is made into this sloping cut about one third of the way down and this forms the tongue. The base of the scion material is then prepared in a corresponding way and the scion is trimmed to include three or four buds. It is slotted into the tongue on the rootstock then the graft is sealed with tape and wax. The buds of the scion should shoot in spring and the strongest one is allowed to develop.

With the grain Describes the way a cut is made through a stem whether it is woody or green. It is made by slicing up or down the length of the stem either to make a slit or a sloping cut.

Wounding Intentionally damaging a part of a plant or cutting in order to expose more of the cambium layer. This encourages callusing and root formation, or the formation of offsets or bulbils when chipping bulbs. Semi-ripe and hardwood cuttings need to be wounded by scoring the base of the cut.

Greenhouses

Alpine house Refers to a glasshouse that attempts to mimic the climatic conditions in alpine regions. This includes ventilation and cooling systems to maintain low temperatures both day and night.

Aspirated screen A reflective metal housing with a fan at one end to draw air through. A thermostat is located inside the aspirated screen and is connected to a heating and/or ventilation system. This piece of equipment has the advantage of rapid response to changes in the environmental conditions via the automated system.

Bench A table-like structure in a greenhouse on which pots of seeds, seedlings, cuttings and plants are placed. The bench can be fixed to the floor and/or sides of the house or can be mounted on rollers so that it can be moved back and forth across the greenhouse. The bench may house some form of heating and/or irrigation system and may be covered in capillary matting or sand to aid the uptake of water by the plant.

Buoyant Describes the environmental conditions within a glasshouse with reference to the balance between ventilation and humidity.

Capillary matting Felt-like material used in greenhouses under pots of plants. If the plant is watered from the top of the pot, any surplus water that drains out of the bottom is absorbed by the matting which then allows the plants to take up this water when needed. Alternatively the matting is used as the watering system and the plants take up water from the bottom of the pot.

Cladding Any material which is used to cover a protected structure. Glass is the traditional and predominant material used although clear polythene, PVC, fleece and other materials are also used. For structures which require little or no light, black polythene or wood is used. Glass allows less transmission of long-wave radiation than PVC and polythene so retains more heat within the greenhouse, which is important during the winter.

Closed case A mini-greenhouse within a greenhouse. It is mainly used for pots of seeds which require a warmer temperature to germinate, and normally consists of a frame with a glass or plastic lid. The lid can be raised to improve ventilation and/or to remove any build-up of condensation. It can also be used for plants which require a higher humidity than the rest of the greenhouse, for example, ferns or cuttings from tropical plants.

CO$_2$ enrichment Supplying a glasshouse or growing area with extra carbon dioxide (CO$_2$). This is normally done with pressurised canisters and fans in order to increase the rate of photosynthesis in some plants.

Cold frame An unheated low structure for hardening off young plants outside. The walls are made of brick, timber or concrete and the front edge is lower than the rear so that the roof slopes forward. The roof consists of two glass panels or lights which slide back and forth to provide ventilation or can be removed completely during the day in warm weather. A cold frame is normally south-facing so that it receives maximum sunlight during the winter, but care must be taken to prevent scorch during the summer months particularly with very young plants. It is also referred to as a frame.

Conservatory Developed from the orangery in the early eighteenth century, when it was fashionable to grow exotic plants and fruits in a protected structure joined to a large and wealthy country house. The roof and south wall of the conservatory were predominantly glass, as they are today, and the conservatory was heated.

Cyclic lighting See *lighting*.

Damping down Wetting the floor of a glasshouse or growing area with water in order to increase humidity and to temporarily reduce transpiration. Sometimes plants are also damped down, especially those with tropical origins or ferns and mosses which enjoy copious moisture.

Evaporation The loss of water or moisture, as it changes from a liquid form to a vapour, due to an increase in temperature.

Frame See *cold frame*.

Glasshouse In the mid-nineteenth century, glass became cheap enough for mass horticultural use as the main cladding material for greenhouses. The term 'working under glass' developed into the term 'glasshouse' which is still used today. It generally refers to a protected structure, usually with glass cladding, which is used to house plants on a large or professional scale. The purpose of a glasshouse is to lengthen the growing or cropping season of a plant, to provide a near-optimum environment for a plant, to grow exotic or tender plants, to reduce environmental damage (although growing under glass may increase pest, disease and disorder damage), and to facilitate the manipulation of the growth of a plant. To this end, glasshouses may contain heating, ventilation and watering systems to control the environment. The term is used interchangeably with greenhouse.

Greenhouse Generally refers to a protected structure, usually with glass cladding, which is used to house plants on a small or amateur scale. The word probably originates from the period when orangeries and conservatories were constructed so that non-native 'evergreens', including citrus fruit, could be overwintered. The term is used interchangeably with glasshouse.

Greenhouse effect Sunlight enters the greenhouse through the glass as short-wave radiation. It is absorbed by the plants, soil and the structure. It then radiates back as long-wave radiation, which cannot pass through the glass, so is reflected back into the greenhouse. This raises the temperature inside and is called the greenhouse effect. Different cladding materials transmit varying amounts of long-wave radiation.

Heated bench A heating system which is enclosed in the bench to supply heat to the base of pots. Base heat encourages and promotes rooting so is often used under pots of cuttings and young plants. Similarly, base heat is supplied beneath pots of seeds because most seeds require a minimum temperature in order to germinate.

Heating Providing heat in a greenhouse particularly during the night, in winter or on cloudy days. Portable heaters which use paraffin, oil or gas are used just to heat an area with minimal control. They can be moved around in a small greenhouse with adequate extractor fans for the fumes. Electric fan heaters are useful for more precise temperature control. In larger greenhouses, water or steam pipe heating systems are used in the floor or under benches or beds and are connected to a thermostat and automated heating system which can be programmed with minimum temperature settings.

Humidity The moisture content in the air. When the level is high it is said to be humid no matter what temperature it is. High levels of humidity within a greenhouse reduce the rate of evaporation and transpiration in the greenhouse and although this is beneficial to most plants on sunny days, certain plants require dry air conditions. High humidity levels can also increase the incidence of certain pests and fungal diseases which thrive in these conditions.

Insulation Materials such as glass, plastic sheeting, bubble plastic and rigid plastic are used to make the insulating panels which line the inside of a greenhouse in order to reduce heat loss and conserve energy. Insulation that is used during the day needs to be balanced with the maintenance of optimum light levels. Thermal screens are specially designed materials which are pulled horizontally across the greenhouse at night to enclose the plants and heating system. This traps the heat and humidity below the screens and they can be pulled back during the day. Most insulating materials also cause condensation and high humidity which can potentially increase the incidence of pests and fungal diseases which thrive in these conditions.

Lath house   A lath is a thin strip or slat of wood, usually from the poplar tree. Lath-houses are constructed out of these slats, or with modern materials, to provide shelter from the wind and temperature extremes, and shade from the sun. They are used to house shade-loving herbaceous plants, for example ferns, particularly in hot climates including the southern states of America.

Lean-to   A half-span greenhouse where the ridge is attached to a permanent wall with the roof sloping down and away for maximum light transmission. It is a popular structure for small gardens.

Light   A pane or panes of horticultural glass with a timber frame. They are the removable part of a cold frame.

Lighting   Artificial lighting within a greenhouse provided in a number of ways to influence the growing patterns of plants. Replacement lighting totally replaces natural sunlight. Supplementary lighting is used in addition to natural sunlight in the morning or evening to lengthen the day and is especially used during winter or on cloudy days. Cyclic lighting switches on and off at regular intervals. Nightbreak lighting maintains equal intervals of darkness to maintain vegetative growth rather than flower development. Photoperiodic lighting varies the quantity and quality of light depending on the time of year and the plant's growth stage.

Mist unit/mist bench   A bench in a greenhouse on which pots of cuttings are placed, where they receive regular automatic misting. Contained within the bench are water pipes which extend up and above the bench at regular spacings. At the top of these pipes are atomiser jets which emit a fine spray of water, or mist, over the pots beneath in short bursts. The frequency of misting can be governed by an electronic leaf which is located on the bench within range of the atomiser jets. Basically, when there is moisture on the electronic leaf the water supply is cut off and when the moisture has evaporated the water supply switches on for a short burst until the leaf is moist again. Therefore, moisture is only applied to cuttings as it is lost from the leaf surfaces, without the saturation of the compost. Mist benches without an electronic leaf can be controlled by manually setting the frequency and duration of bursts depending on the air temperature and humidity at the time of year. In this case, cuttings need to be checked frequently.

Nightbreak lighting See *lighting*.

Orangery   The first type of protected structure consisting of a long north wall with large arched windows on the south side. Orangeries were first built in the seventeenth century primarily to overwinter citrus trees such as oranges. They were still a feature on large country estates in northern Europe during the eighteenth and nineteenth centuries to house other exotic plants.

Overhead irrigation An irrigation system which is raised above the plants or growing area to provide water in the form of a fine spray.

Overwinter   Helping a plant to survive through the winter, if it is not adapted to cool, damp or cold climates, by lifting and bringing it into a protected structure such as a polytunnel or greenhouse.

Photoperiodic lighting See *lighting*.

Pit house   A greenhouse or frame which is sunk into the ground and is usually unheated. It was a popular structure in the nineteenth century for growing exotic fruit and vegetables, for example pineapples, melons and cucumbers.

Polytunnel   A protected structure with a metal frame and polythene cladding. The frame is a series of semi-circular hoops on which the polythene is supported. Polytunnels are generally used to overwinter plants which need some form of protection but do not require the additional heating of a greenhouse.

Protection   Providing a plant with an environment where it can survive during cold, hot, dry or wet periods. Temporary structures or materials can be introduced such as cloches, fleece or shade netting, or the plant itself can be moved inside or outside a greenhouse according to its requirements. Winter protection is important in the UK when cultivating tender plants.

Replacement lighting See *lighting*.

Ridge   The main roofing support structure which runs the length of the greenhouse.

Shading   Providing shade from the sun for the plants in a greenhouse. Blinds can be used internally or externally, but if they are outside the greenhouse less light enters so the temperature inside is reduced further. They can be made out of wooden slats, netting or coloured polythene film, and preferably can be rolled up and down when needed. Alternatively the glass on the outside of the greenhouse can be painted with a white paste mixed with water. This is done in spring and removed in autumn. Shading is important to prevent scorch to the foliage of plants and to reduce the temperature within the greenhouse during the summer.

Sub-tropical   Refers to a glasshouse that attempts to mimic the climatic conditions in the sub-tropical regions. This may include heating to maintain high minimum temperatures (about $16^{\circ}C$) and an irrigation system which mists or waters frequently to maintain high humidity during the growing season.

Supplementary lighting See *lighting*.

Temperate   Refers to a glasshouse that attempts to mimic the climatic conditions in temperate regions. This can include heating and ventilation to maintain even temperatures both day and night, and supplementary lighting to reproduce distinct seasons.

Thermal screen See *insulation*.

Thermometer A gauge for measuring temperature. It is usually glass and contains a cylinder of mercury which expands and contracts with fluctuations in air temperature.

Thermostat   An automated controlling device that measures and regulates temperature levels to a programmed setting. It may activate another device, for example a heating or ventilation system, in order to regulate the temperature.

Tropical   Refers to a glasshouse that attempts to mimic the climatic conditions in tropical regions. This may include heating for high minimum temperatures (about 19°C) and an irrigation system which mists or waters frequently to maintain high humidity during the growing season.

Under glass   Refers to a permanent structure which enables the propagation and the growing of plants. The term is often used to differentiate between seeds that are germinated in a greenhouse rather than in open ground although the structure need not necessarily have glass cladding. Seeds that are sown under glass usually produce earlier crops, and tender plants are raised under glass for protection or to give an extended growing season.

Ventilation   The natural or artificial flow of air through a structure. Excessively high temperatures lead to rapid transpiration and eventual wilting of plants so ventilation is important to allow excess heat to escape from the greenhouse on hot, sunny days. Vents are openings in the sides and roof of the greenhouse and can be manually operated or linked to a thermostat and automated ventilation system which can be programmed with minimum temperatures settings. Vents may also be kept closed to increase humidity. Ridge vents are hinged to the ridge of the greenhouse and are located there because warm air rises. Side vents and louvre vents are positioned on the side walls near to ground level. Electric fans are also a source of ventilation and are useful for reducing stagnant air conditions, particularly on cold and cloudy days when the vents will be closed.

Using plants

Types of plant

Alpine Refers to the habitat from which a plant originates, which is any area above the tree-line on mountains in temperate, sub-tropical and tropical regions. It is also used to refer to other plants which require similar growing conditions.

Annual A plant which completes its lifecycle in one year or growing season. Confusingly, a perennial may be incorrectly referred to as an annual if it is grown only for one year before being discarded. This may occur in bedding schemes or if the plant is a tender perennial.

Aquatic plant A plant which grows with its roots in water as well as most of its other parts. Deep water aquatics are plants which grow with their crown well below the water surface but their leaves and flowers are on or above the surface. Floating aquatics are plants which drift with the current. Oxygenating plants produce vigorous growth predominantly below the water surface. They dissolve many pollutants, take in carbon dioxide and give off oxygen so have major benefits for the health of the water and for the other organisms which live there.

Bamboo A group of plants from the Gramineae family which have cane-like stems and papery leaves.

Biennial A plant which completes its lifecycle within two growing seasons. In the first year it puts on leaf growth and in the second year it flowers, produces seed and then dies.

Bonsai Although technically not a type of plant, it refers to certain miniature trees or shrubs which are the result of a specialised technique of growing so that they are dwarfed. The technique involves stem and root pruning and intricate training and is very popular in Japan.

Broad-leaved Refers to trees which have broad leaves as opposed to conifers which have narrow leaves. Loosely it is used to describe deciduous trees but there are a few evergreen broad-leaved trees.

Bromeliad Members of the Bromeliaceae family which are mainly tropical rainforest epiphytes and, more rarely, mountainous and semi-desert terrestrial plants. A common feature is the rosette formed by the leaves with a central cup for holding water and nutrients. Brightly coloured flowers are borne out of these cups. Air plants are also bromeliads.

Bulbous plant A term that loosely applies to any plant with an underground storage organ, namely bulbs, corms, rhizomes and tubers. They are usually planted amongst perennials in borders and containers to provide colour from their flowers, or naturalised in grassy areas or used as part of a bedding scheme.

Bush A common name for a shrub or large herbaceous perennial.

Cactus (*singular*) **cacti** (*plural*) Members of the Cactaceae family which are stem succulents that store moisture in their swollen stems. The distinguishing features are ribs along the stems, and the flowers, new growth and spines which arise from these ribs.

Carnivorous/insectivorous Describes a plant which traps and ingests insects and other small creatures to obtain nutrients.

Climber A plant with special means of attachment with which to grow up a natural or man-made support. These appendages may be adventitious roots, tendrils, sucker pads, twisting petioles, twisting stems or thorns. A climber can be an annual or a herbaceous or woody perennial.

Conifer/coniferous Usually refers to evergreen trees (and shrubs) which have needle-like leaves as opposed to broad-leaved trees. The term more exactly applies to all trees in the Coniferae group, some of which do not bear cones.

Deciduous Describes a plant which completely or partially dies back for a period of dormancy. The stems and leaves of herbaceous perennials can die back or trees and shrubs may just lose their leaves.

Ephemeral Describes a plant which completes its lifecycle within weeks. This usually gives rise to many generations within one year or growing season.

Epiphyte A plant which grows on the stems and branches of another plant but does not benefit at the expense of the other.

Evergreen A plant whose leaves persist throughout the year. Some of the leaves may die naturally at any time but they are replaced with new ones.

Feathered maiden A two year old grafted tree with laterals.

Fern A primitive division of plants which lack flowers and reproduce by spores instead of seeds. Ferns can be epiphytic or terrestrial, deciduous or evergreen and their notable ornamental feature is their feather-like leaves, or fronds.

Grass Annual or perennial which may be deciduous or evergreen belonging to the Gramineae family. Grasses are grown for their foliage and light-catching inflorescences.

Herb A plant which has culinary, medicinal or aromatic uses. Herbs differ from vegetables because they are used to flavour food or have compounds extracted from them.

Herbaceous Describes plants having soft top growth rather than woody stems. It is generally used to refer to perennial plants which die down to ground level in the winter and produce new growth in spring. The term can also apply to annual and biennial plants but is more often used to describe perennials.

Herbaceous perennial A non-woody perennial which can either be deciduous by partially or fully dying back for a period of dormancy, or evergreen where the stems and leaves persist throughout the year.

Houseplant A plant bought for growing inside the home. It is usually a hardy perennial in its original habitat of tropical, sub-tropical or warm-temperate areas, but in this country it needs the warmth and protection provided by indoor growing.

Insectivorous See *carnivorous.*

Liverwort A primitive plant division where the plants produce spores instead of seeds and depend on water for reproduction. These plants have not evolved water transport systems so are non-vascular.

Maiden A one year old grafted tree with no laterals.

Marginal Describes an aquatic plant which grows with its roots at or just below the water surface, usually at the margins of water.

Medicinal Describes a plant having healing properties whether used in traditional or modern medicine.

Mediterranean A plant originating from the regions which border the Mediterranean Sea which have a warm temperate climate. It is also used to describe plants from other areas with a similar climate of mild winters and hot summers.

Monocarpic Describes a plant which dies after setting seed. Usually applies to plants which live for several years before flowering, setting seed and then dying.

Moss A primitive plant division where the plants produce spores instead of seeds and depend on water for reproduction. These plants have not evolved water transport systems so are non-vascular.

Native A species that grows naturally in the wild of a specific area and has not been introduced by man or other means.

Perennial A plant whose lifecycle covers more than two years and does not die after flowering. The plants can be herbaceous perennials or woody perennials, and both of these can be either deciduous or evergreen.

Plant An all-encompassing term for organisms in the Plantae kingdom which do not have the power to move voluntarily and lack sense organs.

Rambler A plant which grows in a sprawling fashion both upwards and outwards. The term often describes roses which are uncontrolled spreading shrubs. They differ from climbers which tend to grow mainly upwards.

Rock plant   A plant which enjoys growing amongst rocks and in free-draining soil. The term is often used interchangeably with alpine and sub-alpine plants but it also loosely includes plants from coastal and river cliff areas, dry hillside, woodland and pasture areas. They can usually tolerate exposure to the elements but not excessive wet. They are cultivated in rock gardens, raised beds and alpine troughs which can mimic the aspect and soil.

Shrub   A woody perennial with more than one stem arising from the ground. Shrubs can be evergreen or deciduous.

Standard   A tree with three years of lateral growth.

Sub-shrub   Similar to a shrub but is smaller and usually has a shorter lifespan.

Sub-tropical   Describes a plant which originates from the areas in the world between the temperate and tropical zones. These areas have high minimum temperatures and seasonal heavy downpours of rain.

Succulent   A plant that has adapted to extreme conditions, especially frequent periods of drought. Succulents can originate from alpine, semi-desert, temperate, sub-tropical and tropical areas. Adaptations for survival include fleshy, water-storing stems, leaves or roots.

Tender perennial   A plant which in its natural habitat may be a hardy perennial but when it is cultivated in this country it does not survive the colder temperatures so is described as a tender perennial. These plants are normally given winter protection or are grown under glass throughout the year.

Tree   A woody perennial with a single stem known as a trunk. Trees can be deciduous or evergreen. Some shrubs can be referred to as trees if their habit and size are appropriate.

Tropical   Describes a plant which originates from the area in the world between the Tropics of Cancer and Capricorn. These areas have very high minimum temperatures and humidity, and heavy rainfall, either throughout the year or mainly in the rainy season.

Wall shrub   A shrub which can be self-supporting but in cultivation needs the warmth and protection of a wall, or a shrub which needs or tolerates training into a vertical support to foster its growth, or a shrub which is grown and trained onto a wall for a better display of its flowers or fruit.

Weed   Any plant that has seeded itself and is growing in a place where it should not be, as deemed by the gardener. A weed can be any type of plant with any lifecycle. It may be ornamental or have some use elsewhere in the garden, or be ugly or invasive and considered best removed altogether. It is important to note that many British native plants are considered weeds in one garden, whilst in another they are grown to encourage wildlife or to increase biodiversity.

Whip   A one year old tree with no laterals.

Woody   Describes a plant which contains wood in its stems or roots.

Cultivation

Aspect   The direction in which the garden, or part of the garden, faces. For example, if you put your back to the house and look at your garden and you are facing south, then the aspect is 'south-facing'. If you are facing west then the aspect is 'west-facing'. The aspect determines how much sun a garden can get and is therefore important when considering types of plants and their positions.

Cultivation   All of the techniques involved in growing a plant, from the provision of the correct soil, aspect and protection to maintenance such as regular watering and feeding regimes, pruning, dividing, etc.

Dappled shade A position which receives filtered or broken sunlight. The sun's rays may be broken by the foliage of another plant or deliberately filtered by netting.

Deep shade/full shade/shade A position which does not get any direct sunlight and is cast in shadow for most of the day. It may be in a north-facing aspect or have the sun blocked by other plants or buildings.

Direct sunlight/full sun A position which is hit by the sun's rays usually for most of the day. In the garden this will be a south-facing aspect and in the house it will be by a window.

Dormant season/dormant period The period of the year in which the plant is resting, has temporarily stopped growing or is in a period of suspended growth. Dormant periods are different for all plant species. Some may be for less than a month every year and others may be for most of the year with a very short growing season. The length of dormancy is generally governed by climate and habitat, for example, the length of the wet and dry seasons, temperature fluctuations or a change in the day length. This period may vary slightly from year to year due to the particular environmental conditions.

Drought-tolerant Describes a plant which will withstand and survive periods of drought even if it prefers to be grown in more moist soil.

Frost-hardy Describes a plant which can withstand a minimum temperature of -5°C, as a rough guide. The plant will be damaged if the temperature falls below this, so it is usually protected or moved to a frost-free area in severe winters.

Frost-tender Describes a plant which can only withstand a minimum temperature of around 0°C to 5°C, as a rough guide. The plant may be damaged if the temperature falls below this, so it is usually grown under protection for the winter. In milder areas of the UK, the plant may be kept outside with shelter or protection during the winter.

Full shade See *deep shade*.

Full sun See *direct sunlight*.

Greedy Describes a plant which takes up higher than average amount of nutrients from the soil, and therefore demands regular feeding.

Growing season The period of the year during which the plant is actively growing, flowering or fruiting. Growing seasons are different for all plant species. Some may be for less than a month every year and others may be for most of the year with a very short dormant period. The length of the growing season is generally governed by climate and habitat, for example, rainfall, temperature and day length. This period may vary slightly from year to year due to the particular environmental conditions.

Half or part shade/half or part sun A position which gets roughly equal amounts of sunlight and shade. This may be an east or west-facing aspect or have the sunlight obscured for part of the day.

> **TOP TIP**
>
> **Planting against a wall or fence**
> Make sure the root ball is about 45cm away from the support and angle the plant towards it. This gives the roots plenty of room to grow and find moisture away from the dry base of the wall.

Half-hardy   Describes a plant which can withstand a minimum temperature of 0°C (32°F), as a rough guide. The plant will be damaged if the temperature falls below this, so it is usually brought inside for winter, although in milder areas of the UK the plant may be kept outside with shelter or protection.

Hardiness   The capability of a plant to withstand unfavourable weather conditions. It is generally referred to in relation to tolerance of minimum temperatures. Geographical locations and microclimate must be taken into account when considering hardiness ratings because a plant may be hardy, for example, in the south-west of the UK but not in the north.

Hardy   Describes a plant which can withstand a minimum temperature of -15°C (5°F), as a rough guide and so can survive periods of frost.

Invasive   Describes a plant with vigorous growth from the stems and/or roots which can dominate a planted area quickly to outgrow its allotted space. In most cases this causes the death of less vigorous neighbouring plants.

Light shade   A position that is in the shade for most of the day but may still be a bright area because it receives indirect sunlight.

Maintenance   The techniques used to keep a plant at the ideal growth and flowering levels. These include watering, feeding, deadheading, pruning, repotting container-grown plants and lifting and dividing those in the ground.

Moisture-loving   Describes a plant which enjoys having its roots in moist soil. Some can survive with the roots below the water whilst others will die unless the soil is well drained.

Overwinter   Helping a plant survive through the winter, if it is not adapted to cool, damp climates, by lifting and bringing it into a protected structure such as a polytunnel or greenhouse.

Protection   Providing a plant with an environment where it can survive during cold, hot, dry or wet periods. Temporary structures or materials can be introduced such as cloches, fleece or shade netting, or the plant itself can be moved inside or out according to its requirements.

Winter protection is important in the UK when cultivating tender plants.

Provenance The place of origin of a plant. This usually refers to where the seed, cutting or whole plant was collected in the wild.

Season In common language the term refers to one of the four seasons: spring, summer, autumn and winter. Gardeners also refer to one year or one growing period in a year as a season.

Self-seeding Describes a plant which disperses its seed which then germinates and grows with little or no interference from the grower.

Self-supporting This refers to any herbaceous perennial which does not require extra support to stand upright. This may be because it has an erect habit, or because its stems are particularly strong or that old growth persists amongst the new growth to act as support.

Shade See *deep shade*.

Tender Describes a plant which cannot survive cold temperatures and/or frost so it is usually grown under protection for most or all of the year.

Thirsty Describes a plant which takes up a higher than average amount of moisture from the soil, and therefore demands regular watering.

Vigour Describes how quickly a plant grows and fills its allotted space. The term can apply to the root growth or top growth or both.

Wet feet Refers to damp, wet or waterlogged conditions at the roots. Most plants dislike these conditions.

Wildlife gardening Cultivation of a garden to encourage wildlife, normally by using plants which are native and are beneficial to insects, birds and mammals. Usually organic materials and techniques are used.

Design

Accent plant   One which stands out and is prominent in a group of planting. Accent planting is done deliberately to liven up a border by using, for example, an architectural, ornamental or dot plant.

AGM   The Royal Horticultural Society's Award of Garden Merit which is given to species and cultivars which have met a number of criteria in plant trials. Panels of experts look at ornamental characteristics, constitution, pest and disease susceptibility, maintenance requirements and propagation issues before giving this award to the best performers.

Anchor plant   A plant which helps to merge other plants with the ground, such as low-growing shrubs or ground covering plants.

Architectural plant   A subjective term for a plant which has a strong or bold form, habit or texture.

Autumn colour   Refers to the vibrant colours on a plant during the autumn season, either from the leaves turning shades of orange and red or from the colour of the berries.

Bed   A planted area which can be viewed from all sides.

Bedding   A group of plants that are temporarily grown en masse for a colourful display. Annuals, biennials and tender perennials are normally used and then discarded at the end of the flowering season.

Border   A planted area which can be viewed from one, two or three but not all sides.

Canopy   The aerial part of stems and leaves as a whole, particularly in trees.

Carpet bedding   A type of bedding whereby low-growing plants are grown very close together to create a carpet of flowers or foliage, sometimes in the form of colourful images.

Climbing/scandent The upward growth habit of a plant either by special means of attachment or twining stems.

Clump-forming The growth habit of a plant which has the stems and foliage radiating upwards and outwards from the basal clump which usually increases in girth each year.

Container Any receptacle which will hold soil and can be planted in, including pots, baskets, boxes, troughs, etc.

Culinary Edible or flavouring property.

Cushion-forming/mound-forming Describes the growth habit of a plant where the stems and foliage are densely packed and grow close to the ground.

Dot plant A tall plant which is grown singularly or in groups in a bedding scheme in order to add height.

Double flower A flower with more petals than in the normal wild species.

Drift A large group of planted species which is meant to appear natural by being planted in long swathes and intermingled with other species.

Edging Plants which make up the planting at the edges of borders and beds, mainly in reference to bedding schemes.

Evergreen A plant whose leaves persist throughout the year. Some of the leaves may die naturally at any time but they are replaced with new ones.

Fastigiate The habit of a plant, mainly trees, where the stems and branches grow upright at angles to the main stem.

Focal point A plant or feature which draws the eye. To be used as a focal point, a plant would need to have strong form and habit all year round.

Foliage The leaves.

Form The three-dimensional shape of a plant, for example, columnar, conical, spiky, dome-shaped or round. It is easier to see the form of a plant when all its leaves are showing.

Formal A term used in garden design to describe the style of a garden. It usually applies to gardens with strong symmetry, and geometric shapes with straight lines and edges. The planting can also be set out in this manner with shrubs and hedges being clipped tightly.

Functional plant One which is grown for a purpose, such as for wildlife, for shade, for eating, for medicinal purposes or to act as a hedge.

Ground cover Any plant or planting which is low-growing so that the foliage covers the ground. This conserves soil moisture and suppresses weeds.

Groundwork Plants which make up the majority of planting in a border, especially with reference to bedding schemes.

Growth habit The visual characteristic of a plant due to the direction and manner in which it grows.

Habit The two-dimensional growth shape of a plant, for example, weeping, tortuous, fastigiate. It is easier to see a plant's habit without its leaves.

Ha-ha A deep and wide ditch dividing a cultivated area from a field or natural land to prevent animals from entering. It is constructed so as not to be visible from the house, usually a manor, or similarly large country residence.

Hard landscaping Everything in the garden that is not the plants, lawn or soil, for example, paths, gates, walls, water feature or patio.

Hedge A dense barrier formed usually from shrubs or trees which have been planted close to one another.

Herbaceous border A border which is predominantly planted with herbaceous plants but may contain some shrubs and bulbs.

In the green The stage of growth of a plant, usually a bulb, after it has finished flowering but before its foliage withers and dies back.

Informal A term used in garden design to describe the style of a garden. It usually applies to gardens which are in direct contrast with formal gardens. They have less defined spaces with flowing curves and the planting is less restricted and managed.

Knot garden A tradition from the Middle Ages of setting out an area in geometric beds, each one enclosed by low-growing neat hedges in intricate patterns. Lavender and box were commonly used for the hedges whilst herbs were used for planting in the beds.

Mat-forming Describes the growth habit of a plant where the stems and leaves form an impenetrable carpet close to the ground with little upward growth.

Mixed border One which is planted with a mix of shrubs, herbaceous perennials and sometimes annuals.

Mound-forming See *cushion-forming.*

Naturalise The process of planting in a permanent position and then allowing the plant to increase its numbers by natural means. It often refers to the manner in which bulbs are haphazardly planted, especially in areas which are less cultivated, so as to give a natural effect.

Ornamental plant A plant which has notable features, usually the flowers, but it can be coloured bark or leaves, odd-shaped fruit or decorative seed heads.

Parterre A formal garden laid out in a series of partitioned areas, usually divided by low-growing shrub hedges and containing flowerbeds. It is a tradition which originated in France in the seventeenth century.

Planting plan A scaled drawing of an area which is to be planted, showing exactly where the plants are to go and the numbers to be planted.

Plunge Sinking a potted plant into the soil so that the rim is at soil level or just above. Plunge planting is used either to keep the plant's root growth restricted, or to protect the roots from hot and cold temperatures, or for easier watering of that specific plant. It also allows a plant to be lifted easily and brought inside over winter, especially tender perennials which have been temporarily planted in bedding and border schemes. It is also employed if a plant requires different soil conditions from the plants in the surrounding border.

Prostrate The growth habit of a plant which grows horizontally along the ground.

Rosette-forming Describes the growth habit of a plant where the foliage radiates out from the crown and is usually densely packed.

Scandent See *climbing*.

Season of interest The period of time during which the plant has notable features.

Seed head A fruit which contains the seeds and is usually referred to when it is dry and is held aloft by the plant on the old flower stems. Seed heads can be an ornamental feature of a plant.

Shelterbelt A planted belt of trees and shrubs which provide shelter from wind, noise or pollution to a garden.

Single flower A flower with the normal amount of petals for that species as opposed to a double flower.

Soft landscaping The plants, lawn and soil in the garden, as opposed to the hard landscaping.

Specimen A plant which is grown singularly and prominently due to it having superior or special features. It may also be grown amongst other plants to act as a focal point.

Spring bedding Bedding which flowers over the spring season. Commonly spring-flowering bulbs are interspersed amongst the other plants.

Standard A tree or shrub which is pruned to leave a clear singular stem on which the branches and foliage are held in a round shape for ornamental effect.

Structural plant One which has a strong presence in the garden and acts as part of the backbone for the garden. Structural qualities may be, for example, evergreen, dense foliage or height.

Summer bedding Bedding which flowers over the summer season. Commonly summer-flowering bulbs are interspersed amongst the other plants.

Texture The overall visual roughness or smoothness of the plant due to its leaf size and shape. Small or narrow-leaved plants are said to have a fine texture and large-leaved ones to have a coarse texture, which is important when designing a planting scheme. The term also describes the feel of the leaf surface, for example, rough, velvety, smooth, prickly.

Tortuous   Describes the habit of a plant where the stems have many twists and turns so that the plant is contorted.

Underplanting Plants which are grown under the canopy of a tree or shrub. The plants which are used for underplanting are preferably at their best when the trees and shrubs above do not have any leaves, for example, spring-flowering bulbs or perennials under deciduous trees.

Variegated   A leaf which is not all one colour. They may be more or less one colour such as shades of green, purple or golden with stripes, blotches or mottling of another colour such as white, cream, purple, etc.

Water garden One which contains a body of water, whether natural or manmade, pond or stream. The plants surrounding the water should be moisture-loving or tolerate water at their roots, whilst the plants in the water should be aquatics and/or oxygenating plants.

Weeping   The habit of a plant where most of the growth hangs down from the main framework.

Wild garden   One which mimics the plants and planting associations in a wild habitat. It can either be cultivated to any degree or left to its own devices.

Windbreak   A structure which impedes the flow of wind, for example, trees, shrubs and fences. This reduces soil erosion, heat loss, evaporation and plant damage to the leeward side.

Woodland garden One which mimics the plants and planting associations in a woodland habitat.

Practical
gardening

Soil preparation

Ameliorate   Improving the soil by any means, including digging and adding organic matter.

Bed   A planted area designed for viewing from all sides, so is usually surrounded by lawn or paths.

Border   A planted area designed for viewing from one, two or three sides, so usually has a boundary on one or more sides.

Cap   A hard horizontal layer of soil on the soil surface through which roots cannot grow. A cap is produced by compaction after heavy rain or by walking on wet soil and can be broken up by hoeing or lightly forking the surface. See also *pan*.

Clod   A lump of soil where the individual particles or crumbs are bound together.

Consolidate   Making the soil stable by lightly compacting it to a lower level usually after digging. This is done by evenly treading over the soil using the weight over your heels.

Crumb structure   The condition of the soil and how the individual crumbs are bound together. Ideally it should not be too sticky or dusty. Cultivating the soil in the right conditions can improve the crumb structure but equally over-cultivation can ruin it.

Cultivate   The true sense of the word means to mechanically break up the soil but can also include the practice of adding organic matter and tending to the soil as in weeding and feeding.

Dig   Turning over the soil using a spade or fork.

Double dig   The spade is pushed fully into the soil (one spit deep) and this amount of soil is removed and taken to the end of the plot. This is continued along the land so that a trench is formed, the base of which is forked over to a depth of one spit more and organic matter can be incorporated. This process is repeated so another trench is formed adjoining the first but the soil that is removed can be used to refill the first trench. This process is continued until the entire area has been dug. The final trench is filled with the soil removed from the very first trench. This system is also known as 'bastard trenching' for obvious reasons!

Drill A continuous narrow slit made in the soil into which seeds are sown or seedlings planted. The depth of the drill will vary according to the seed but is usually 2cm to 5cm deep.

Fork over Turning over the soil using a fork in order to relieve compaction or break up soil capping. This is done during the season when digging is not necessary.

Furrow A continuous narrow trench made in the soil into which seeds are sown or seedlings planted. The depth of the furrow will vary according to the seed and this term normally applies to larger scale farming rather than horticulture.

Grubbing up Clearing the ground of roots and stumps.

Levelling Ensuring the soil is level to receive seeds or plants by pulling a rake back and forth over the soil.

Mulch Placing a layer of material, the mulch, on the surface of the soil and around plants to conserve moisture, suppress weeds and improve the soil structure. It can be organic, for example, compost, straw, bark, or inorganic, for example, gravel.

Pan A hard horizontal layer of soil either on top of the soil or beneath the surface through which roots cannot grow. A surface pan, or cap, is produced by compaction after heavy rain or by walking on wet soil and can be broken up by hoeing or lightly forking the surface. A sub-surface pan is caused by cultivating to the same depth over a long period and can be broken up by double digging.

Raised bed A bed that has been raised above the normal level of the ground and may have retaining sides. Soil and/or organic matter is introduced to build up the bed, which can be of better quality or a more preferable pH level than the original soil. Other benefits are that plants, especially vegetables, can put down deeper root systems so they can be grown closer together, and that the soil temperature is warmer, meaning plants can be grown earlier and develop quicker.

Raking   Pulling the soil back and forth with a rake to level it off or to break the soil down into a finer tilth.

Ridging   A variant of single digging whereby the third spit of soil that is removed is then placed on top of the previous two spits. This creates a ridge and a furrow every third spit. It is a method of soil cultivation in areas of heavy soil and high rainfall as it increases the surface area of soil for weathering and also improves drainage.

Seedbed   An area of soil that is ready for seed sowing. It needs to be weeded, dug or forked over, consolidated and raked into a fine tilth with any large stones removed.

Single dig The spade is pushed fully into the soil (one spit deep) and this amount of soil is lifted and turned back into the hole. If this is done in autumn, the clods are usually left to be broken down by the elements over winter to produce a finer tilth by spring.

Tilth   The fine and crumbly texture of the soil surface produced by cultivation or by natural weathering.

Trench   A continuous slit cut into the soil. A deep trench can be dug for planting trees and shrubs for hedges, or a shallow, flat-bottomed trench can be made with a draw hoe for sowing multiple lines of seed.

Trenching   This is similar to double digging except that one further spit of soil is removed before forking over the base of the trench.

Weeding   Eradicating annual and perennial weeds from the soil either by manually removing them with a fork or grubber or by slicing through the top layer of the soil with a hoe. Herbicides can also be used for chemical removal.

Planting

Anti-transpirant A foliar spray designed to reduce transpiration.

Backfill Refilling the planting hole with soil once the plant is in place.

Bare root Trees, shrubs and roses can often be purchased in this form. They have been grown in an open site, dug up and the bare roots temporarily wrapped in hessian or plastic.

Base dressing A fertiliser that is applied to the soil prior to planting, either at the bottom of the planting hole and therefore at the base of the roots, or incorporated into the soil during preparation. A base dressing is an initial feed, as opposed to a top dressing.

Container-grown A plant which has been grown in a container at each stage of its life and is purchased in this form.

Crock Coarse material placed under the plant's roots at planting time to aid drainage. Broken clay pots are a favourite material. Crocks are usually only used for container growing.

Dividing The practice of splitting one plant into two or more pieces. Each division must have the potential of roots and shoots in order to survive. The reason for dividing a plant is either to increase the stock of that plant, or to remove an unproductive area of the plant (usually the centre in herbaceous plants) or to reduce the size of a plant which has outgrown its allotted space.

Dormant The period in which a plant is at rest and not actively growing or flowering. It is best to

> **TOP TIP**
>
> **When planting a container-grown plant**
> Tease out the roots from the base and sides of the root ball, this will give the roots and plant the best start.

purchase and plant at this time, generally November to March in the UK.

Firm
Pushing the soil down into the planting hole and around the roots once the plant is in place. This stabilises the plant, settles the soil and reduces air pockets.

Heel in
A temporary measure to protect the roots of a plant when it cannot immediately be set into its permanent position. The plant is usually laid on the soil and the roots covered with soil and gently firmed in.

Lift
Prising a plant out of its growing position, taking all or most of the roots with it. For small plants a fork can be used but with larger plants, shrubs and trees it is best to dig around the plant with a spade first to expose the root ball.

Mulch
Placing a layer of material, the mulch, on the surface of the soil and around plants to conserve moisture, suppress weeds and improve the soil structure. It can be organic, for example, compost, straw, bark, or inorganic, for example, gravel.

Naturalise
The process of planting in a permanent position and then allowing the plant to increase its numbers by natural means. It often refers to the manner in which bulbs are haphazardly planted, especially in areas which are less cultivated, so as to give a natural effect.

Nursery bed
A temporary bed for raising young plants. Seeds may be sown there, and the seedlings allowed to grow on until they are large enough to be moved to the permanent planting bed. They are commonly used in vegetable plots when space is restricted.

Nursery mark
The level in the soil at which the plant was grown in the nursery. The mark can normally be seen at the base of the stem as it is darker where it was under the soil. A plant should always be replanted at the same level with a few exceptions.

TOP TIP

Lightly water a seed bed before you sow fine seed

The seeds will then stick to the soil rather than float away. The same applies for compost in a pot or tray.

Puddling   After placing a plant into its planting hole, the soil surrounding it is watered so the soil falls back in around the roots. Some plants prefer this gentle method of backfilling, especially if they resent root disturbance.

Ridge planting A method of planting in raised ridges rather than at the normal soil level. This is to provide better drainage, especially for plants which are prone to rotting at the collar, such as strawberries and some vegetables. It also allows soil to warm up more quickly so that these plants can develop earlier in the season.

Root ball   The mass of roots and soil bound together on a plant.

Root zone   The area of soil that contains the roots and the surrounding soil into which the roots may grow.

Seedling   A young plant which has germinated from seed and either has only the seed leaves or the first true leaves (this is open to interpretation depending upon the size and age of the plant).

Top dressing A fertiliser which is applied to the top of the soil and left to be washed in by water. A top dressing is normally scattered around plants in subsequent years after planting, as opposed to a base dressing. Other materials can also be applied as a top dressing, for example, grit, gravel or compost, to improve drainage, to reduce diseases or for ornamental purposes.

Transplant   Moving a plant from one growing position to another. The term can also apply to the actual plant that is being moved.

Water in   Watering a plant once it has been planted, ensuring it is given enough water to reach all of the roots and settle the soil.

Wind-rock   The movement of a plant by the wind which can lift the roots or damage the plant. This can be reduced by planting to the correct depth, firming the plant in well and possibly staking a large plant.

Pruning and training

Annual pruning Pruning which really needs to be done every year either so that the plant is kept under control or to the desired shape, or so that it produces maximum flowering or fruiting wood.

Batter The slope of a hedge created by clipping so it is thinner at the top and fatter at the bottom to give it more stability and to allow more light to the base.

Break Growth from a bud on a stem which has been pruned.

Climber A plant which has a special way of attaching itself to a support in order to grow upwards. In the wild the support is a neighbouring tree or shrub and in the garden we can provide support by means of a wigwam, a fence with wires or bamboo canes and string. Without this support the plant will grow along the ground. The plant attaches itself by adventitious roots, sucker pads, tendrils, thorns, twisting petioles or twisting stems. A climber can be herbaceous or woody, annual or perennial.

Clip Giving a plant a light trim all over usually with hand shears. Used to create topiary.

Congested Describes when there is a lot of growth in a particular area of a plant so that the twigs or branches touch, cross or rub together, which can damage the plant. This usually occurs in the centre of a shrub where branches can be selectively pruned out.

Coppice Cutting trees back to ground level to produce several vigorous new stems. Each subsequent cut is taken back to the developed stool. A technique used on trees which produce wood which is economically viable, for example, willow for basket weaving.

Dead head To remove any finished flowers on a plant. The whole flower and the pedicel is usually cut away.

Formative pruning The process of pruning in the early years of a plant in order to develop a basic framework.

Framework The permanent structure of a plant, either where the positions of the branches are natural or where they have been manipulated through pruning.

Frame-working Pruning all growth back to the main framework and then grafting a different cultivar onto the branches of the main framework.

Hard prune Generally means to cut back to the ground or just above it or back to the main framework. This varies according to the plant in question and can refer to all growth or just this season's growth but is normally done once a year.

Heading back Pruning of all stems of a plant by one third to one half of their length.

Hedge A row of closely planted trees or shrubs which form a dense mass either as a boundary, barrier or partition. They are usually regularly cut to a certain height and width in order to keep the shape and density.

Last/previous season's wood The stem growth which was produced in the previous year's growing period. It is darker and woodier than the current year's growth.

Leg The stem on a plant below the main branches. Lower branches may be removed to create a leg on shrubs and fruit bushes.

New wood Stems which are less than one year old.

Old wood Stems which are more than one year old.

Open centre Created by removing some or all of the wood growing through the middle of a plant. This improves air circulation, allows more light to penetrate through the plant, helps to ripen wood and reduces the occurrence of disease.

Outward/upward facing bud A bud which points towards the outside/top of the plant and will produce a stem which grows in that direction. It is useful to prune to just above one of these buds so that the plant will grow outwards/upwards and not get congested.

Pinch out Removing the growing tip of any stem on a non-woody plant to encourage more growth from the side shoots.

This is usually done on young plants to produce a bushy habit or to provide more material for vegetative propagation.

Plashing   A training technique to form a type of dense hedging whereby branches are bent down and woven back into the plant.

Pleaching   A pruning and training technique on trees to form a type of hedge, screen or avenue. Starting at about one metre up the trunk, branches are trained horizontally and then at a number of levels until the desired height is reached and then the leader is pruned out. All lateral growths are spur pruned back to the horizontal branches every year to maintain the shape.

Pollard   Regularly pruning all branches back to the trunk of a tree which then produces new shoots. This technique is used a lot on street trees to save time on maintaining their size.

Primary branches The branches which grow from the trunk and which make up the basic framework of a plant.

Prune   Cutting and removing any amount of a plant especially trees, shrubs and climbers. This is done in order to remove dead, damaged and diseased wood, to remove branches which are crossing or rubbing, to change the shape or size of a plant, to create an open centre, to encourage new vigorous growth, flowers and fruit, to prevent excessive wind-rock, to remove growth which shows reversion or is too weak, and to produce new growth which shows better colour in the stems or leaves.

Renovation/renewal pruning Pruning of an overgrown or neglected plant by removing a third of its wood, leaving a third and tipping a third over a number of years until the plant has replaced itself with new growth and is restored either to its

> **TOP TIP**
>
> **Bamboo, hazel and willow**
>
> If you have a bamboo, hazel or willow in your garden, cut a stem whenever you need a plant support or cane. Alternatively harvest the stems every year in spring as new stems will grow back.

allotted space or becomes productive again with flowers and/or fruit.

Restricted A term given to trees and shrubs which are trained in some way, for example, to a wall or wires.

Routine pruning Pruning which is done at regular intervals in order to keep the plant under control or to the desired shape, or so that it produces maximum flowering or fruiting wood.

Rub out Literally to rub the buds off a stem with your fingers to stop them from developing.

Secondary branches The branches which grow from the primary branches and which make up the basic framework of a plant.

Spur pruning Cutting this season's lateral stems to two remaining buds. This produces lots of stumped twigs which look like spurs.

Staking Providing upright support to a plant by tying it to a post or cane which is driven into the adjacent ground.

Stool A tree stump or clump of basal shoots from which new shoots will grow.

Stopping Removing the main growing tip of any plant to encourage more growth from the side shoots.

Stressing Training a stem by bending it before tying it into the support structure. This 'stresses' the plant, encouraging it to produce certain growth hormones which encourage it to produce more flowers and/or fruit.

Sucker A shoot growing from a stem or root below the ground. Plants that use a different rootstock cultivar often produce suckers from the rootstock which are obviously different from the plant above ground.

This/current season's wood The stem growth which was produced in the current year's growing period. It is greener and more pliable than the previous year's growth.

Tipping Removing the tip end of any stem from a woody plant to encourage more shoots to be produced further down the stem.

Topiary Refers to the art of clipping and sometimes training a shrub into shapes such as spheres and cones and more eccentrically into shapes of animals. The term also refers to the end product.

Training   A way of keeping a plant in place and manipulating its growth in a certain direction.

Trim   Really depends on what is being pruned but generally means a very light cut all over, perhaps anything from one to five inches off.

Unrestricted   A term given to trees and shrubs which are not trained but are left free-standing.

Wall shrub   Either a shrub which enjoys a bit of warmth and protection from a wall or fence and is free-standing, or a shrub which needs or tolerates being tied in and having an annual prune. Also applied to shrubs which have a show of flowers or berries which are better displayed when trained against a wall.

Wood   Refers to any stem growth. It may be a new, green and pliable stem or an old, brown and woody branch.

Lawns

Aerate   Making holes in a lawn to introduce air to the root zone of the grass, in order to improve drainage and relieve compaction. It is best done in autumn either manually with a garden fork or with a powered aerator or tiner.

Amenity lawn   Lawn which is used for a variety of leisure purposes and takes a lot of wear.

Autumn feed   Fertiliser which is applied to a lawn in the autumn and generally contains more phosphorus to promote strong roots and potassium to harden up the grass over winter and promote good disease resistance.

Bent   Describes a number of grass species which are hard-wearing and drought-resistant and tolerate close mowing.

Blade   One leaf of grass.

Clippings   Grass cuttings from mowing.

Cultivated turf High quality turf produced for sale by sowing light sandy soils with a variety of grasses.

Cumberland turf Turf which comes from marshy areas and has been sea-washed. It contains fine grasses and is mainly used for high quality sports areas like bowling greens.

Downland turf   Turf which comes from chalky areas and is a mixture of mainly fine grasses.

Drought-resistant Describes a grass or mix of grasses which can tolerate lack of water over a period of time without dying.

Edge   Cutting the blades of grass which hang over a lawn and onto a border using edging shears.

Fescue   Describes a number of grass species which are quick to establish, are drought-resistant and tolerate close mowing.

Grass	Plants in the Gramineae/Poaceae family. Certain species are used to create lawns as an evergreen ground cover plant which tolerates constant cutting and grows densely so as to discourage weeds.
Hard-wearing	A grass or mix of grasses which tolerates a lot of traffic.
Irrigation	Watering system, usually sprinklers are used for watering lawn.
Lawn	A grassed area in the garden which is kept mown.
Lawn fertiliser	Normally a balanced mix of the main nutrients applied to the lawn in the form of granules (see autumn and spring feed).
Laying turf	The practice of creating a lawn by placing sections of turf onto an area of prepared soil. Each section of turf is laid tightly against the next, so that the join can knit together. Each row of turf is laid in a staggered fashion (as bricks are laid) to reduce the number of joins at any one point.
Leaching	The loss of nutrients due to excessive watering or rain washing them through and out of the soil.
Lifting turf	The practice of removing a grassed area by slicing horizontally through the soil just beneath the grass roots and then lifting so as to remove a whole turf section. A turfing iron is the best tool for this job but a spade will suffice.
Luxury lawn	Lawn which is rarely used but is more of an ornamental feature. It needs to be well cared for and requires a lot of maintenance.
Meadow turf	The cheapest turf you can buy which can contain weeds and coarser grasses but is sufficient for a utility lawn.
Mow	Cutting the lawn with a lawn mower.
Rye	Describes a number of grass species which are very hardwearing and good for a utility lawn.
Scarify	Raking the surface of a lawn to remove thatch and moss and to stimulate the growth of tillers. It is best done in

> **TOP TIP**
>
> **Use the fertile molehills on your lawn**
> Shovel off the earth and spread it onto beds and borders. It won't get rid of the moles but then what does!

autumn either manually with a springbok rake or using a powered scarifier.

Sheath A protective covering which encloses part of the stem and leaf base on grasses and is usually thin and papery.

Sod The term for turf in the USA.

Spike Making holes in a lawn in order to aerate it.

Spring feed Fertiliser which is applied to a lawn in spring and generally contains more nitrogen to promote leaf growth and a good colour.

Sward The collective term for the amount of grass blades in an area of lawn. It can be likened to the term carpet 'pile'. A dense sward is ideal.

Thatch The layer of dead grass and tillers above the soil and beneath the live grass blades.

Tiller A side shoot arising at the base of a stem. Cutting grass encourages the formation of tillers and produces a denser sward.

Top dress The application of a sand and loam mix to the surface of the lawn to improve the structure of the soil and fill small indentations in the lawn. Top dressing does not have a fertilising effect but can improve drainage on clay soils and moisture retention on sandy soils. It is best done in autumn especially after aeration or on newly lain turf and the dressing should be lightly worked in with a besom broom or loot.

Turf A rectangular section of grass with the roots matted in a thin layer of soil which has been lifted for re-laying elsewhere. Also an interchangeable term for lawn.

Utility lawn Lawn which is used for a variety of leisure purposes and takes a lot of wear.

Worm-cast The wiggly bits of soil on the surface of a lawn which are the waste products of worms.

Fruit and vegetables

Fruit

Bark-ringing/ringing Removing bark around the circumference of a trunk or branch on a fruit tree. The ring should be about 6mm wide and left incomplete with about one third of the bark intact. This reduces vigorous vegetative growth above the ring and helps to increase the yield of fruit.

Biennial bearing A tree which produces a crop every other year with little or no flowers and fruit in the intervening years.

Bloom A natural protective coating on fruit such as grapes and plums which appears powdery or waxy.

Breastwood Stems that grow out from the main framework when fruit trees are trained against a wall or wire system.

Burr knotting The eruption of adventitious root initials from trunks and branches of predominantly old apple species. They appear as knarled masses and indicate the rooting potential of the tree. They are not harmful to the plant and can be left or cut away.

Bush fruit Fruit grown on a shrub which has been pruned for the first two to three years to produce a clear leg of around 10cm to 15cm, about eight to ten main branches and an open centre. Pruning from then on maintains this bush shape for maximum fruit yield and ease of harvesting. Gooseberries, redcurrants and blackcurrants are all usually grown as bush fruit.

Bush tree A tree which has 60cm to 75cm of stem and is pruned to produce an open-centred shape.

Cane Growth produced from suckers at the base of a plant. The term is widely used concerning raspberry and blackberry growth.

Citrus fruit Sub-tropical fruits from the Rutaceae family such as orange, lemon and grapefruit. They need warmth and shelter and the frost protection of greenhouse or conservatory in the UK.

Cordon   A tree which has been pruned to leave a single stem with spurs. A vertical cordon is left upright and an inclined cordon is trained to about 45°.

Crop   The fruit that is produced at one time or over a period and which is harvested.

Double worked A grafting technique whereby a rootstock is grafted to an intermediary scion which is then grafted to the fruiting scion. This is used with fruit trees such as pears when the rootstock and fruiting scion are incompatible as a normal graft.

Early crop   A crop produced earlier than the normal harvesting season for that particular crop.

Espalier   A tree with a vertical main stem which has been tipped to produce laterals which are then trained in horizontal tiers.

Family tree   A grafted fruit tree which has two or more scions from different species or varieties, and therefore produces two or more different species or varieties of fruit. The scions are from the same family and this technique is mainly used with apple trees.

Fan   A tree which has been pruned and trained to produce a fan shape. The leader of the tree is pruned to about forty centimetres above at least two buds. These produce laterals, two of which are trained either side to 45° and the following year are pruned to about 30cm. This produces more laterals which are trained in at angles either side, thus producing a fan shape after about three years. Any unwanted lateral buds are rubbed out.

Festooning   Restricting the flow of sap to discourage vegetative growth and encourage fruit production. Branches are bent into severe curves in the summer when they are pliable and either tied onto the main stem or weighted to the ground.

Flower set   The successful development of a flower which is receptive to sexual reproduction.

Framework   The basic stem and branch structure of a tree either created naturally by growth or manipulated by pruning and training.

Fruit	The structure which contains the seed, and in this case it is that structure which can be harvested and partly or wholly eaten. Fruit plants are normally perennials.
Fruit set	The successful development of fruit after pollination and fertilisation.
Fruiting cane	A cane which is old enough to produce fruit or one which has produced fruit.
Fruiting spur	A spur which will produce flowers and fruit.
Fruitlet	A small immature fruit.
Girdling	Removing a complete ring of bark around the circumference of a trunk or branch on a fruit tree. Alternatively, something is tied tightly around the limb. Both methods restrict water and nutrient flow so that the parts above the ring finally die.
Goblet	A tree which has been trained into the shape of a goblet. It has a short trunk from which the branches are firstly trained outwards and then upwards and held by a hoop to keep the shape.
Harvest	Collecting the mature ripe fruit from a plant. It also refers to the period of collection.
Harvest interval	The period of time between spraying pesticides onto a crop and being able to safely harvest that crop.
Head	The part of a tree growing above the trunk.
Late crop	A crop produced later than the normal harvesting season for that particular crop.
Leg	A trunk created on a shrub by removing lateral branches at the base. The purpose of a leg is to hold the 'bush' higher above the ground.
Main crop	The crop of fruit which yields more than earlier or later crops from the same plant. The term also applies to the variety or cultivar which produces such a crop.
Mature	A fully developed or ripe fruit.
Mid-season crop	Produced in the middle of the normal harvesting season for that particular crop. On seed packets and in catalogues, the term also applies to the variety or cultivar which produces such a crop.
Orchard fruit	A generic term for all fruit which is produced by trees, with or without pruning and training. Apples, pears,

plums and cherries are all orchard fruit. This term is used interchangeably with top fruit.

TOP TIP

Frost pockets
Avoid planting fruit trees or early flowering trees in frost pockets otherwise the blossom and fruit may be ruined.

Organic   Compounds which contain carbon. Also refers to gardening and producing crops by using organic materials only and thus without the use of synthetic chemicals as found in most pesticides and fertilisers.

Partial tip bearer A fruit tree which produces most of its flowers and fruit at the tips of the young and old shoots but may also produce some on spurs.

Pip fruit   A fruit which has the seed or seeds surrounded by a fleshy tissue with no stone. The pips can be enclosed on the inside as in apples and pears or on the outside as with strawberries and raspberries. The whole fruit is usually edible.

Pollinator graft A graft where a scion from a fruit cultivar, which is particularly free-flowering and produces abundant virile pollen, is grafted to another cultivar of fruit tree within the same genus, so that pollination is increased in the main cultivar. This is often used on crab apples and in orchards.

Primocane   A cane during its first year of growth when it flowers and fruits in its second year.

Pyramid tree A tree which is pruned over a couple of years so that the head is a pyramid shape.

Restricted   A term given to all fruit trees and bushes which are trained in some way, for example, to a wall or wires.

Ripe   A fully developed fruit at its best for harvesting or eating. The fruit should come away from its stalk easily and the flesh will be sweet and fully coloured.

Rootstock   A plant which is used for its root system to which a scion is grafted to produce a grafted tree or shrub. The rootstock may provide a short stem or the entire trunk with or without a part of the branch framework. The rootstock and scion are usually the same species but may be different cultivars. The rootstock is used to control one or many of the characteristics of the fruit-bearing species, namely vigour (hence the term dwarfing), fruit size, age of maturity, time of ripening and the crop rate. It may also affect the resistance to disease or whether the fruit stores well. The rootstock may also possess better anchorage or uptake of nutrients than the grafted species.

Soft fruit A generic term for fruit which is produced by a plant other than a tree. For example, raspberries are produced on canes, gooseberries on shrubs, strawberries are herbaceous perennials and grapes come from vines.

Spawn When talking about canes, the spawn is the young growth which is less than a year old.

Spindle tree A fruit tree which is pruned to produce a series of laterals which decrease in length up the trunk to produce a Christmas tree shape. These laterals are then weighted to the ground so that they are horizontal.

Spur A lateral stem which has been pruned to two buds. The resulting short branch looks like a spur.

Spur bearer A tree which produces most of its flowers and fruit on spurs.

Step over A single-tiered espalier.

Stone fruit A fruit where the seed is enclosed within a stone and then surrounded by fleshy tissue which is usually edible. For example, apricots, plums and mangoes are stone fruits.

Stool A clump of basal canes. As old, fruited canes are pruned down, new canes are produced and the stool enlarges.

Suckering The production by a plant of new shoots from the root which emerge above ground close to the parent plant. This is normally an unwanted process with ornamental and fruit trees but with fruit such as raspberries it creates fresh growth for subsequent fruit.

Thinning The selective removal of fruitlets when they are small so that the remaining ones have room to develop into larger fruits especially on grapevines and plums where the fruitlets are tightly packed together.

Tip bearer   A tree which produces its flowers and fruit mainly at the tips of young and old shoots but not from spurs.

Top fruit   A generic term for all fruit which is produced by trees, with or without pruning and training. Apples, pears, plums and cherries are all top fruit. This term is used interchangeably with orchard fruit.

Training   A technique of tying in branches or stems to a wall or wire system so that a basic framework is created and the stress created on the stems encourages more flower and fruit set. Training also allows more sunlight to reach the fruit for ripening, makes harvesting easier and provides a pleasing display in ornamental gardens.

Tropical fruit Fruit from tropical plants which are considered exotic in temperate climates.

Unrestricted   A term given to all fruit trees and bushes which are not trained but are left free-standing.

Vine   A grapevine, the plant which produces grapes as the fruit. A vine can mean any climbing plant in the USA.

Weaving system A training method normally used for blackberries and similar fruits. The canes are led up and under a series of horizontal wires so that the fruiting briars are together and the new vegetative growth is separate which makes pruning and harvesting easier. There are various methods of weaving which can create some very ornamental patterns.

Yield   The amount of fruit obtained from a plant.

Vegetables

Blanch Stopping light from reaching the stems and leaves to keep the crop soft and not tough and stringy, for example, with celery and rhubarb. Different materials can be used, including upturned clay bells, plastic drainage pipes and soil.

Bolting This can happen when a plant starts to produce growth that will flower and set seed. The growth is rather too rapid and the stems become long or leggy in order to hold the flowers aloft. Vegetables grown for their leaves like lettuce and cabbage have a tendency to do this in hot weather and the crop is deemed unfit if it starts to bolt and does not produce a good heart.

Bolt-resistant Cultivars which have been specially bred to resist the tendency to bolt which is of course a natural process. The benefit is that the plant produces more leaves which can be harvested.

Brassicas A group of vegetables which come from the Crucifereae family and the Brassica genus. They include broccoli, Brussels sprouts, cabbage, cauliflower, kale, kohl rabi, swedes and turnips. They all require high amounts of water and nitrogen to help produce their leafy growth.

Bulb vegetable A general term for vegetables from the Liliaceae family including onions, garlic, spring onions, shallots and leeks. Bulbs need fertile soil but are not as demanding as the brassicas. This term is used interchangeably with onion family.

Catch crops Crops which take a short period of time to reach maturity for harvesting and so are grown on areas of ground which are waiting for the main crop.

Clamp A store to preserve root vegetables after harvesting by mounding up straw and soil over the roots to protect them from frost.

Cleaning crop A crop which is grown over an area of ground which would otherwise be bare. The foliage of the crop acts as ground cover to suppress weeds and the roots break the soil down into a good crumb structure.

Collar A piece of material that is placed around the stem of the plant and lies on the soil surface. It helps prevent insects from laying their eggs in the soil surrounding the plant so that the emerging larvae hopefully do not chew through the stems.

Crop The vegetable or part of a vegetable that is produced at one time or over a period to be harvested and eaten.

Crop rotation A devised system of growing different groups of vegetables on a plot of land every year. The groups can be loosely divided according to family such as legumes, Solanaceae, brassicas, Umbellifereae or onion, or based on what part of the plant is to be harvested such as seed, shoot, fruit, root, leaf or bulb. In reality only three or four groups are selected and rotated one after the other on the plot of land. A common system is to grow root vegetables, followed by legumes, followed by brassicas followed by bulbs. Crop rotation reduces soil-living pests and diseases, which will reach epidemic proportions if allowed to thrive on one crop. It also helps to keep soil nutrients balanced as one crop will deplete the soil of a particular nutrient over time.

Cucurbits Vegetables belonging to the Cucurbitaceae family such as marrows, squash, cucumbers, courgettes, pumpkins and gourds. They all need a long warm growing season to ensure that the fruits can ripen.

Curd The densely packed, immature flowerbuds which make up the heads of broccoli and cauliflower. It is these that are eaten.

Cut and come again Vegetables which can have all or some of their leaves harvested time and again over the season.

Deep bed system The vegetable plot is laid out in beds with narrow paths around the edges. Double digging and the incorporation of organic matter ensure a deep root zone encouraging the crops to draw their nutrients from greater depths so that they can be planted closer together.

Early   A crop that is produced earlier than the normal harvesting season for that particular crop. The term is also given to the variety or cultivar which produces such a crop.

Early sowings Seed sown earlier than is recommended by giving it some kind of protection in order to allow it to germinate and grow on. Early sowings can be made in the greenhouse before being moved outside, or under cloches in situ. This technique gives these plants a head start and extends the harvesting season for that crop.

Earth up   To draw soil up around the base of a plant. This can be to encourage the formation of roots from the stem as with potatoes, or to blanch the stems as with leeks, or to help prevent windrock with top-heavy plants such as sprouts.

Eye   An undeveloped growth bud on a tuber, as for example on potatoes.

Fleecy film/floating fleece Lightweight fleece which is placed over seeds, young seedlings or a crop to act as frost, wind and pest protection, whilst allowing water and light to pass through. The fleece can be weighted down or pegged at the sides, and the plants lift the fleece as they grow.

Floating mulch This is usually black polythene which is placed on the soil surface as a mulch. It warms the soil at the start of the season, suppresses weeds and acts as a barrier against pests. Plants can be grown through the polythene by slitting the plastic.

Fruiting vegetable A vegetable which is grown for the fruit to be harvested such as tomato, aubergine, pepper and chilli.

Green manure A crop which is grown on an empty plot of land specifically to be dug into the ground to add organic matter and nutrients. It is usually grown over winter and dug in in the spring. Whilst the plants are growing they also suppress weeds, break up the soil and improve drainage. Good plants for green manures are from the Leguminoseae family, such as broad beans, which can fix nitrogen in the soil.

Harvest   Collecting the part of the plant which is to be eaten. It also refers to the period of collection.

Harvest interval The period of time between spraying pesticides onto a crop and being able to safely harvest that crop.

Haulm The leaves and stems of vegetable plants, and the term especially refers to the top growth of potatoes and legumes.

Heart up A natural growth habit in vegetables such as cabbages and lettuces. There is little stem growth so that the leaves grow close together to form a tightly packed heart with the older outer leaves folded over the new inner leaves.

Heart/head The compact mass of leaves in vegetables such as lettuce and cabbage and the densely packed florets in broccoli and cauliflower.

In situ In the permanent growing position. Seeds can be sown in situ as opposed to in a greenhouse, seed bed or nursery bed.

Inorganic Compounds which contain synthetic chemicals not derived from living or dead animals and plants. Also refers to gardening and producing crops by using inorganic materials.

Intercropping Growing of crops which take a short period of time to reach maturity for harvesting. These crops are grown between rows of the slower-growing main crop to make full use of that space.

Late A crop that is produced later than the normal harvesting season for that particular crop. The term is also given to the variety or cultivar which produces such a crop.

Leaf vegetable A vegetable which is grown for its leaves to be harvested such as kale, chard, spinach, sprouts and cabbage.

Legume Refers to vegetables from the Leguminoseae family which produce pods such as beans and peas. Legumes have a special and important characteristic in that

TOP TIP

Second cabbage crop
Spring and early summer cabbages can be made to provide a second crop. After you have harvested the main head, make a shallow cut (13mm deep) on the top of the stalk and small heads will develop from the edges of the cut.

they have nitrogen-fixing root nodules which help to replace that nutrient in the soil. The top growth of legumes can be dug into the soil after harvesting as a green manure. Because of this, brassicas are usually grown on this land in the following year, as they require high quantities of the nutrient nitrogen to produce their leaves.

Lifting The technique of forking the crop up and out of the soil so as to harvest the roots. The term also applies to any plant that is being taken out of its growing position.

Long-term crop A crop which takes a comparatively long time to reach maturity. Most brassicas are long-term crops and are usually sown in seedbeds or nursery beds and then transplanted into their permanent positions later in the season so that this land can be used for earlier crops.

Main crop The crop which yields more than earlier or later crops from the same plant. The term also applies to the variety or cultivar which produces such a crop.

Mature A fully developed plant or fruit. With vegetables the term is used to describe the plant when the part which is to be harvested is ready or ripe.

Multiple seeding/sowing To sow a number of seeds in one position. The intention is to thin out the weaker seedlings once they have germinated or to leave the vegetable seedlings to grow into a clump where they can push for space but still produce a good crop, for example with radish and onion.

Nursery bed An area of ground which is set aside specifically for raising seedlings and young plants before they are planted out in their permanent positions. The idea is that they need less space at this stage and do not require thinning so it is an efficient method of producing larger crops such as the brassicas.

Onion family A general term for vegetables from the Liliaceae family including onions, garlic, chives, shallots and leeks. This term is used interchangeably with bulb vegetable.

Organic Compounds which contain carbon derived from living or dead animals and plants. Also refers to gardening and producing crops by using organic materials only and thus without the use of synthetic chemicals which are found in most pesticides and fertilisers.

Potager   An ornamental vegetable plot. The bed patterns are designed to be decorative as well as functional and the vegetables are usually chosen for both their ornamental and edible qualities.

Root vegetable A vegetable which is grown for the root to be harvested such as carrot, parsnip, radish, turnip, beetroot, potato (which botanically is a tuber) and swede. Root vegetables help to create good soil structure and drainage for the following crop.

Run to seed   A vegetable which has flowered and produced seed and is normally deemed past its best for harvesting. This is the natural lifecycle of the plant although vegetables are normally harvested before this takes place so that the crop remains palatable and the energy of the plant is focused on the part to be eaten rather than setting seed.

Salad vegetable Any plant which can be used in salads but usually refers to the quick growing crops which take up little space such as lettuce, radish, cress, endive and chicory.

Seed potato   Not the seed of the potato plant, but a potato itself which has been certified virus-free and is a healthy tuber which is chitted and planted.

Seed vegetable A vegetable which is grown for the seed to be harvested such as peas, beans and sweetcorn.

Seedbed   An area of ground which is set aside specifically for raising seedlings. They are sown closer than the recommended spacings, before being transplanted to their permanent positions. This is an economic way of using the ground and ideally cuts down on the amount of discarded seedlings due to thinning.

Sets   Onions, shallots and potatoes which are used as seed.

Shoot vegetable A vegetable which is grown for the shoots to be harvested such as celery, asparagus and Florence fennel.

Short-term crop A crop which takes a comparatively short time to reach maturity. Most salad vegetables are short-term crops and are sometimes used as intercrops or catch crops.

Solanaceae family The main vegetables which belong to this family are potatoes, tomatoes, aubergines and peppers and these are grouped together in the crop rotation system. It is otherwise known as the potato family.

Sow thinly To sow seed in a continuous line in a drill or over the entire surface of soil rather than place deliberately in a set position. The important factor is that they have enough space to germinate without too much competition but can be thinned to the correct spacing once they are seedlings. This usually applies to smaller seed such as those from the Umbellifereae family.

Spacing The ideal distance between seeds and plants to allow the seeds enough room to germinate and the plants to fully develop to their optimum size. The term is used when sowing seed and planting out and also for the distance between rows.

Standing quality The ability of a crop to withstand the elements when they are still growing and ripening. It is an important factor with crops that mature over the winter and long-term crops which may suffer wind-rock and heavy rain.

Station sow To sow seed in deliberate set positions along a drill or bed. Individual seeds or a group of seeds may be placed at set distances apart. This usually applies to larger seeds such as legumes.

Strip bed system A traditional vegetable plot whereby the vegetables are sown and grown in long rows with narrow paths in between. Now it is mainly used in commercial growing.

Strip cropping Moving cloches, polytunnels and fleece from one strip of vegetables to the next at their critical growing or fruiting stages to gain maximum yields from each crop.

Successional sowing Sowing seeds of the same crop repeatedly through the season. This ensures a constant supply of that crop and hopefully avoids gluts. It also prevents the whole crop being wiped out by adverse weather conditions or pests.

Support Any method of keeping the plant upright or growing in a way to improve crop production and to ease harvesting. Canes and string are a popular method of support.

Thinning	The process of selectively weeding out excess seedlings of a crop so that the remainder can develop to their optimum size. This is normally done when more than enough seeds have been sown. The weak or damaged seedlings are preferably taken out, ensuring that those that are left are at the ideal spacing for growth.
Thirsty	A term given to plants that require more than average amounts of water to produce a good crop.
Umbellifereae	The main vegetables which belong to this family are carrots, parsnips, celery and parsley.
Vegetable	A generic term for any plant which is grown to be harvested and eaten. Vegetables differ from fruit and herbs in that they are normally annuals or biennials.

Pests and
diseases

Pests

Adult   The last stage of an insect's lifecycle. It emerges from the pupa in the fourth stage of complete metamorphosis and develops from a nymph in the third stage of incomplete metamorphosis. The adult insect rarely does much damage to plants but flies about looking for nectar and a mate. The adult mollusc, mite and nematode do as much plant damage as their young.

Ant   A social insect which lives in nests in the soil and can be winged or wingless. Ants occasionally eat small pieces of leaves and remove seeds from pots and open ground for food for their larvae. They also cause damage to roots by tunnelling underneath which can lead to the plant wilting, and the mound ant causes aggravation by throwing soil up over the nest especially on lawns. Ants also farm aphids, scale and mealybug for their honeydew, so whilst not directly damaging the plant the ants encourage the spread and maintenance of these other pests.

Aphid   Small sap-sucking insect which is from 1mm to 5mm long with a soft body, relatively long legs and antennae and a pair of tube-like limbs at the end of the abdomen. It is commonly white, green or black in colour but this may extend to other colours. It has piercing and sucking mouth parts, and the aphid feeds almost continuously on the sap of the host plant causing weakening and distortion of new growth. Aphids are vivaporous and breed rapidly by parthenogenesis. They can quickly become a serious infestation at the height of breeding because the mother aphid can give birth to live young, who themselves contain live young! They excrete honeydew which falls onto leaves and stems below and encourages sooty mould. Aphids also transmit viruses from diseased plants to healthy ones.

Beetle   A member of the largest order of insects which is characterised by modified forewings which form hard wing covers over the abdomen. It has a relatively small head with antennae, large eyes and strong mouthparts which can bite and chew soft and hard food. It is usually brown, black or grey but is sometimes brightly coloured. It lays eggs which become maggot-like larvae near to a food source. Both the adult beetle and the larvae can prey on other insects or small invertebrates so can be beneficial to the gardener, or feed on dead wood or feed on living plants. Examples of pest beetle larvae are the chafer grub and wireworm, and examples of a pest beetle are vine weevil and lily beetle.

Beneficial insect An insect which does not cause damage to a plant and may actually benefit the plant, the soil and the garden in general. For example, the hoverfly, butterfly and bee are all beneficial insects because they are prolific pollinators of flowers. The lacewing and ladybird are beneficial because they feed on aphids, a major pest in the garden and greenhouse. The stag beetle is beneficial because it feeds on dead and decaying wood which in turn benefits the soil.

Blackfly   A species of black aphid.

Caterpillar   The larvae of moths and butterflies. The head has a pair of strong jaw-like mouthparts which are used to bite and chew plant tissue. The thorax has three pairs of jointed legs and the abdomen has up to five pairs of fleshy legs. The size and colour of caterpillar species varies. Moths and butterflies feed on nectar and lay their eggs on or near plants. The larvae then hatch and feed for a couple of months before pupating and emerging as adults after a few weeks. Some caterpillars and pupae overwinter in the soil and plant debris. Most gardeners will find caterpillars chewing through leaves, buds and shoots on ornamental plants, fruit and vegetables, although they do feed on all parts of the plant.

Centipede   Often confused with a millipede but only has one pair of legs per segment and moves rapidly. It is a beneficial insect because it is mainly carnivorous, feeding on small insects, slugs and other invertebrates.

Chafer grub   The larvae of the chafer beetle which lives in soil especially in grassland and overgrown gardens. Most gardeners will find the chafer grub underneath turf. It has a soft, white, curved body up to 40mm long, with a brown head and three pairs of legs. It mainly feeds on roots but also stems, causing wilt and death of the plant.

Cranefly   See *daddy-long-legs.*

Cutworm   A caterpillar of various moths which lives in the soil and feeds mainly at night. It eats the stems of plants at ground level and often cuts right through, hence the name.

Daddy-long-legs   The common name for the crane-fly which has a long narrow body with three pairs of over-sized legs and a pair of wings. They are not harmful to plants in this adult stage but the larvae, leatherjackets, do much damage. Daddy-long-legs can be found in damp warm weather in summer and early autumn flying just above lawns and meadows.

Earwig   An insect of up to 25mm long with a pair of horny pincers at the rear of the abdomen. The earwig hides in flowers during the day and then eats the petals at night although it also attacks leaves and buds. It can often be found hiding in wounded fruit but rarely damages the fruit itself. It does most damage from June to September.

Eelworm   A microscopic worm-like creature also known as a nematode. It is about 1mm to 2mm long, living in soil, water, animals and in living and dead plants. The plant-attacking species punctures tissue cells and extracts the fluid contents. It causes discoloration, distortion and death of the plant and the eelworm can also transmit viruses. It can attack a number of ornamental and vegetable plants.

Egg   A capsule containing an undeveloped young animal which will hatch into a larva or nymph.

Fly   An insect with one pair of functional wings and a pair of club-shaped balancing organs to the rear. The size of a fly can vary from 2mm to 40mm but it is always characterised by a large head with prominent eyes, antennae and piercing and/or sucking mouthparts. The adult fly rarely feeds on plants except occasionally on nectar but the main damage is done by the larvae which are legless and colourless maggots. The larvae of some fly species feed on plant tissue, for example, the narcissus fly, carrot fly, crane-fly and some leaf miner and midge larvae. They can cause extensive damage to different parts of the plant.

Gall mite A mite which induces the host plant to produce a gall in which the mite lives. The gall is a conspicuous malformation which can be seen as a raised lump on leaves. In most cases, neither the gall mite nor the gall does serious damage to the host plant and control is often unnecessary.

Gall wasp A small insect of up to 8mm in length with two pairs of wings, long antennae and long dark bodies. The adult female lays her eggs mainly in buds and leaves and the larvae develop within a conspicuous gall which is produced by the host plant. Neither the gall nor the gall wasp does much damage to the host plant although growth may be stunted in younger plants.

Greenfly A species of green aphid.

Grub The larvae of beetles.

Hermaphrodite Bearing both male and female sexual organs in one body as, for example, with slugs.

Honeydew A sticky substance excreted by aphids, mealybug, scale insects and whitefly. Honeydew is the excess sugars and water from the sap on which they feed.

Host The living plant, or plants, which provides the pest with the most suitable home and/or food.

Insect A cold-blooded invertebrate animal which has a hard external skeleton. The body is segmented into the head, thorax and abdomen and it has three pairs of jointed legs. It has one pair of antennae, specialised mouthparts for feeding, and most species of adult have wings. Insects are classified into orders according to their appearance and lifecycle. More than half of insect species use living plant material as food at some stage in their lifecycle.

Larva (*singular*) **larvae** (*plural*) The young insect which hatches out of an egg and is the second stage of complete metamorphosis. Larvae look dramatically different from the adult insects, and are often plump and worm-like in appearance. Maggots, caterpillars and grubs are all larvae. The larva spends most of its time feeding before metamorphosing into a pupa.

Leaf miner A caterpillar of some species of moth and butterfly, which tunnels into leaf tissues in order to feed. The tunnelling is usually visible as whitish squiggly lines on the surface of the leaf or as brown blisters. In most cases the leaves go brown or shrivel up and prematurely drop from the plant.

Leafhopper A sap-feeding insect between 3mm and 10mm long. The adult has powerful hind legs with which to jump if disturbed and this can often be seen on plants during the summer. The eggs are laid in the leaf veins and the nymphs feed on the underside of the leaves and cause a white mottling on the upper surface of the leaves. Leafhoppers also spread bacterial and viral diseases.

Leatherjacket The larva of the crane-fly or daddy-long-legs which is greyish-brown and up to 5cm long. It feeds on the roots and stems of seedlings and older plants, which turn yellow and wilt. It is particularly common beneath lawn which can turn yellow in patches. Most damage is done in the autumn when the larvae emerge from eggs, and in the spring and summer before they pupate.

Lifecycle The development of insects from the birth of an egg to the death of an adult which can involve complete or incomplete metamorphosis.

Lily beetle A bright red beetle which mainly attacks lilies.

Maggot The larva of flies.

Mealybug A small sap-sucking insect of up to about 4mm long. The female is the most common and is wingless and oval in shape with minute legs around the edges. The body is soft and covered in a white powder and waxy filaments. The female lays batches of eggs, each batch covered by a white, woolly wax like candy-floss. Once they hatch they can crawl over the plants to feed. They can be found on any part of a plant, and especially on the growing points, in heated greenhouses and on houseplants. The infestations weaken the plant and foul the leaves and stems below the colony with honeydew.

Metamorphosis The series of changes in the shape and form of an insect during its lifecycle. Complete metamorphosis involves four stages from egg to larva to pupa to adult, for example in butterflies, beetles and flies. Incomplete metamorphosis involves three stages from egg to nymph to adult, for example in aphids and whitefly.

Millipede A pest of sorts which has up to fifty segments with two pairs of legs per segment. It moves slowly and smoothly and some species curl up into tight coils. It lives in the soil and leaf litter and predominantly feeds on dead and decaying plant material. However, millipedes do sometimes feed on seeds and seedlings, bulbs, corms, tubers and roots as well as strawberry fruit. They can also worsen any wound by burrowing deeper and eating the soft tissue.

Mite A small creature resembling an insect but with four pairs of legs on a small body which is less than 2mm long. Some mites feed on plant tissues and are considered a serious pest because they breed rapidly and are less easily controlled by chemicals than other pests. The most common mite to be found in the greenhouse is the red spider mite which forms large colonies and spins a mass of threads over the plant. Both the young and the adults feed on the sap and produce mottling on the leaves.

Mollusc A group of animals including octopus and cockles, and the plant pests slugs and snails.

Moth A butterfly-like creature, but often less brightly coloured. The winged adult moth itself does no damage to plants and in fact can help pollination as it feeds on the nectar within the flowers. It is the larval stage, or caterpillar, of the moth which attacks plants.

Mouthparts Most insects do damage to plants by feeding on whole parts of plants or by extracting plant sap and this depends on their mouthparts. An insect can have two mandibles which are hard and jaw-like mouthparts which are used for biting and chewing plant parts such as leaves. Some insects have stylets which are sharp tube-like mouthparts which are used to pierce and suck plant sap. The stylet punctures plant tissue and the insect either pumps out the fluid or allows the sap to enter the stylet by the plant's natural sap pressure. Thrips possess rasping and sucking mouthparts in the form of short stylets which abrade the plant surface allowing the thrip to suck the contents.

Nematode   See *eelworm*.

Nymph   The young insect which hatches out of an egg and is the second stage of incomplete metamorphosis. The nymph resembles the adult insect apart from the lack of wings. The nymph spends most of its time feeding before developing into the adult insect.

Parasitic   Describes an organism which lives on or in another organism from which it obtains food but gives no benefit in return.

Parthenogenesis The development of an unfertilised egg by asexual reproduction and therefore the species does not require the male for reproduction. This occurs, for example, in aphids, gall wasps and vine weevils.

Pest   An animal which in some way can harm part or all of a plant. Pests can be classified into vertebrates (with backbones) and invertebrates (without backbones). The former includes birds, rabbits, moles, squirrels and deer, and the latter includes insects, mites, molluscs and nematodes.

Pupa (*singular*) **pupae** (*plural*) The third stage of complete metamorphosis when the larva moults and changes into a non-feeding pupa which is often surrounded by a hard cocoon shell. The pupa can take weeks or months to metamorphose into the adult insect.

Red spider mite See *mite.*

Sawfly   An inconspicuous insect of up to about 10mm long which looks like a flying ant. The female cuts into plant tissue to deposit her eggs which then hatch into larvae. The larvae look like caterpillars but have at least six pairs of fleshy legs. It is the larvae which do the damage to the plant by rapidly stripping vast quantities of leaves. Some sawfly larvae are characterised by holding their bodies in the air whilst feeding.

Scale insect   Small sap-feeding insect which produces a white or brown waxy scale of up to 5mm long over its body. It remains fairly static on a plant surface and feeds by inserting its fine tube-like mouthparts into plant tissue. It is common on trees in the UK and in tropical greenhouses. The female lays hundreds of eggs under a protective wax scale or woolly wax. All growth stages of the scale insect feed on sap and also excrete honeydew.

Slug   A soft-bodied mollusc which moves on an undulating and muscular slimy foot. It feeds mainly on leaves with its rasping mouthpart creating holes. It also feeds on all other parts of many different plants, and young plants are the most susceptible. It feeds at night and leaves a glistening slime trail. The adult lays clusters of spherical white eggs which can often be found in rotting vegetation in spring and summer. It is a close relative of the snail and differs by the lack of a shell which means that slugs can move through and live in soil.

Snail   A soft-bodied mollusc with a conspicuous hard shell into which the body can retract. It moves on a muscular slimy foot. It feeds mainly on leaves with its rasping mouthpart creating holes. It also feeds on all other parts of many different plants, and young plants are the most susceptible. It feeds at night and leave a glistening slime trail and the adult lays clusters of spherical white eggs which can often be found in the soil over winter. Snails require calcium for their shells and so are most common on calcareous soils or gardens with mortar in the walls.

Symptom   The effects of a pest or disease organism on a plant. Symptoms are visible to the gardener either as changes to the plant organs, for example, discolouration of leaves, or to the plant itself, for example, wilt and death.

Thrip   A small cylindrical insect up to 4mm long. The adult is commonly known as a thunderfly and has two pairs of narrow wings. Colour varies from white to grey to black and the larvae resemble the adult without the wings.

Both the larvae and the adults feed on plants by rasping mainly the leaves and sucking the contents. Most thrips can be found on the undersides of leaves and a silvery mottling is apparent on the top surface of the leaves. Most damage is done to young plants although established plants can suffer distortion and be weakened. Thrips enjoy hot and dry conditions in the greenhouse.

Thunderfly A common name for the adult thrip.

Vector An organism which transports and transmits a pathogen from one plant to another.

Vine weevil See *beetle* and *weevil*.

Viviparous A reproductive ability of some insects to give birth to live young rather than lay eggs.

Wasp A large insect of up to 20mm in length with yellow and black banding. It is less plump and hairy than a bee. Wasps cause most damage when feeding on ripening fruit in the summer and can also extend damage caused by other pests. They can also scrape and chew the stems of some plants to make their nests by mixing the plant tissue with their saliva.

Weevil A type of beetle which varies in size from 2mm to 25mm long. It is characterised by a projecting snout at the front of the head with the mouthparts at the end. The antennae are usually jointed like an elbow and the three pairs of legs are conspicuously jointed. The larvae are soft white maggots with a well-developed head. Both the adults and larvae feed on dead and living plants, in particular cutting semicircular pieces out of leaves. The vine weevil is fast becoming a common pest in the UK. The larvae are white with brown heads and feed on roots and the base of stems, often unnoticed until the plant falls over. The adults feed at night and cut notches out of leaves.

Whitefly Small sap-sucking insect up to 2mm long and characterised by a white body with a pair of white wings that fold back over the entire body when at rest. The adults, eggs and nymphs are present on the underside of leaves, and leaf surfaces at a lower level are covered in honeydew. Infestations reduce plant vigour and the honeydew encourages sooty mould. Glasshouse whitefly is widely established in greenhouses in the UK, and other species occur on vegetables and on certain weeds.

Wireworm

The larva of the click beetle which can flick itself into the air when lying on its back. The larva is about 25mm long and a golden-brown colour. It lives in the soil and feeds on potato tubers as well as on the roots of many vegetables and ornamental plants.

Woodlice

Grey, segmented, land-living crustaceans which live in decaying organic matter. This is their main food although they will also eat through seedling stems and other parts of larger plants. They hide during the day under wood, stones, pots, etc. They are widespread in neglected gardens.

Diseases and disorders

Bacterial disease A disease caused by a bacterium which lives in or on living plants.

Bacterium (*singular*) **bacteria** (*plural*) A micoscopic, single-celled organism which lives on or in living or dead organisms. Most bacteria are saprophytic so are beneficial in the decomposition process, but some are parasitic, causing a variety of plant diseases.

Black spot See *spots*.

Blackleg The blackening of the base of a plant stem caused by a number of fungal or bacterial diseases.

Blight Fungal and bacterial diseases which cause the rapid collapse or withering of plant parts.

Cane blight A type of canker disease which commonly affects raspberry canes.

Canker A bacterial or, more commonly, a fungal disease which attacks woody plants and causes the death of the cambium tissue under the bark. The disease gives rise to a lesion where no new bark forms, known as the canker. The fungus enters through a wound or natural opening, and the mycelium then spreads to kill the bark and cambium just beneath. The fungus usually spreads each year so the lesion widens, and if the canker extends around the entire circumference of the twig, branch or trunk then die-back occurs above the lesion. Coloured pustules which are the fruiting bodies of the fungus may appear on the canker. Different bacteria and fungi species cause different types of canker.

Chlorosis The blanching or yellowing of leaves due to a nutrient deficiency. Lime-induced chlorosis is a deficiency in iron and is characterised by the yellowing of the youngest leaves but not the veins. It is so called because iron is often rendered unavailable in alkaline soils derived from limestone.

Club root   A fungal disease which mainly affects plants from the Brassicaceae/Crucifereae family and is seen most frequently on vegetables from that family. The fungal spores can remain in the soil for up to twenty years and when they germinate they invade the roots of the host plant causing the roots to swell and become distorted. These swellings are known as galls and when the roots die the spores enter the soil again. The plant can wilt and recover at first but then becomes stunted as the disease worsens. The foliage can be tinted red-purple but characteristically the roots are swollen, usually into one large gall.

Coral spot   A common fungus which is mainly saprophytic and therefore found on dead wood. It occasionally attacks live wood through wounds and can cause canker and die-back. In both cases, it is characterised by a mass of salmon-pink pinheads called pustules on the wood.

Corking   Describes when part of a plant turns woody, like cork. This usually occurs on roots or fruit due to erratic watering or a nutrient deficiency.

Cracking/splitting Describes when part of a plant splits open and can either form a callus or a disease may enter the wound. Cracking is usually due to erratic watering or a nutrient deficiency and most usually occurs on fruit or roots.

Damping off   The rotting of seedlings at soil level which then die off in patches. It is caused by a number of fungal diseases, mostly soil-living.

Deficiency   See *nutrient deficiency.*

Die-back   The gradual death of stems or branches from the growing tips down the plant. It is normally caused by a number of fungal diseases and differs from the rapid die-back caused by wilt.

Disease   An ailment of a plant caused by fungi, bacteria or viruses. All these biological pathogens are parasitic and infectious. The disease can manifest itself as abnormal size, shape or structure of the plant or plant part, or as a malfunction of the plant or plant part.

Disorder   A harmful condition of a plant caused by nutrient deficiencies or environmental conditions. Disorders are non-biological, non-parasitic and non-infectious. The disorder can manifest itself as abnormal size, shape or structure of the plant or plant part, or as a malfunction of the plant or plant part.

Distortion   The abnormal growth of parts of plants, especially the leaves and flowers, which results in twisted, puckered and generally strange shapes. This is normally a symptom of pest, bacterial or viral attack but may also be due to phytotoxic damage.

Dollar spot   A fungal disease which causes rot on lawns, especially on red fescue grass. The grass dies in roughly circular patches and appears yellow-brown in colour with thin dark banding on the leaves.

Downy mildew An off-white or slightly purple mould produced by a number of fungi species. Plant parts which are coated with downy mildew usually turn yellow, shrivel and sometimes die, causing the plant to weaken and, in severe cases, die. Downy mildew is not related to powdery mildew although the symptoms may appear the same.

Dutch elm disease A fungal disease which attacks elm trees and causes wilt. The fungus is transported around the tree by the vascular systems, it then blocks these systems and produces a toxin which is transported to the leaves which turn yellow and brown, shrivel and die as a result. The whole branch and then the entire tree dies. It is rare for a tree to survive an attack. The fungal spores are spread from infected trees to healthy ones by the elm bark beetle which burrows under the bark to lay eggs.

Facultative   Describes a parasite which possesses the ability to live on dead as well as living matter.

Fairy ring   A rough circle, of any diameter, of mushrooms or toadstools which are the fruiting bodies of a fungus. It is the result of a fungal disease which starts at one point in the soil and gradually radiates outward. The fairy ring is usually the only visible sign of the disease and is most apparent on lawns in the spring or autumn.

Fasciation The distortion of a stem so that it is flattened as if it has been squashed, or gives the appearance of being two stems that have joined. There is some mystery over the cause of fasciation. Some experts believe that it is due to pest damage, while others put it down to pollution and others claim it to be a viral cause.

Fireblight A canker which is caused by a bacterial disease which attacks many woody plants from the Rosaceae family. The bacteria enters blossom and then spreads down the stalk to the spurs and branches. The blossom dies, the leaves turn brown and branches appear to have been scorched by fire, hence the common name. There is often associated slime apparent on the affected parts and the plant can die rapidly. The bacteria can be spread by rain splashes, insects and birds.

Fruiting body A structure of fungi which bears the spores, for example, mushrooms and toadstools.

Fungal disease A disease caused by a parasitic fungus.

Fungus (*singular*) **fungi** (*plural*) Organisms which are primitive plants without chlorophyll so cannot photosynthesise. They rely on organic matter for their energy and carbon. Fungi can be parasitic, saprophytic or symbiotic.

Gall A swelling or abnormal growth caused by a fungal or bacterial disease and also by eelworms and mites. It causes little damage when it occurs on leaves and stems and may be pruned out, but can seriously weaken a plant if the gall occurs on the root. Crown gall is a common example, especially on fruit trees, and is found at the join between the root and stem. It is thought to be caused by a bacterial disease. Club root is also a gall, caused by a fungal disease on brassicas.

Grey mould A mould which is characterised by grey fluffy growth which is usually present on buds, flowers and flower stalks and is sometimes accompanied by stem and leaf rot. The fungus spreads rapidly in the air and persists in the soil and on plant debris.

Honey fungus A fungal disease which causes die-back and rot on almost all woody plants, although it mainly affects trees. A number of fungi species cause honey fungus and it is one of the most important plant diseases. The fungus lives in dead tree stumps and the rhizomorphs, which looks like black bootlaces, spread through the soil to infect neighbouring healthy trees. Spores from the toadstools of honey fungus can also spread the disease by entering freshly cut surfaces on vigorous trees or stumps. The first symptom of infection is the die-back of leafy branches or the failure of leaves to emerge in spring. Die-back usually then progresses rapidly. Other characteristic symptoms of honey fungus are death of the bark at the base of the tree, whitish sheets of mycelium occurring beneath the bark, a strong mushroomy smell, resin oozing from the base of the stem, black strands that look like bootlaces in the soil surrounding the tree, and toadstools. These toadstools are generally a honey or tawny colour and appear in autumn at the base of the tree. The roots of the infected plant develop a brown rot which turns stringy and white, and this can spread up the trunk for about half a metre.

Host The plant, or plants, which provides the pathogen with the most suitable home and/or food.

Hyphae Microscopic thread-like structures which make up the mycelium in fungi and spread out to find food.

Leaf curl A fungal disease which produces the unequal expansion of leaf tissue, causing the leaves to pucker. A number of fungi species cause different types of leaf curl. Some fungi produce coloured blisters on the leaves. Plants which are infected usually survive although they are weakened. Leaf curl that occurs on peaches and almonds is the most serious and the curling is accompanied by a reddening of the leaves and a bloom which covers the infected leaves. Repeated attacks causes premature leaf-fall and the tree becomes weak and fruit production declines.

Leaf spot See *spots*.

Lime-induced chlorosis See *chlorosis*.

Marbling/mottling Flowers or leaves which show a mottled effect in a different colour to the normal colour. This is often a symptom of a number of diseases and disorders.

Mosiacs Viral diseases which cause the symptom of yellowing leaves in angular shapes around the veins. In monocotyledons the yellowing is in the form of streaking. Mosaics rarely kill plants outright but can weaken them.

Mottling   See *marbling*.

Mould   A fungal disease which is widespread on many plants. A number of fungi species cause different types of mould and the symptoms are varied with black, grey, green or white mould occurring on any part of the plant, for example, grey mould and sooty mould.

Mushroom   An example of a fruiting body of a fungus. It is born above ground on a stem with a parasol-like cap which contain the spores for reproduction. The mushroom is often the only visible sign of the fungus by which identification is possible.

Mycelium (*singular*) **mycelia** (*plural*) The vegetative body of fungi consisting of branched root-like structures which smell mushroomy or mouldy.

Necrosis   Death of plant tissue. This can be small spots or patches on leaves or fruit, or the stalk of a leaf or flower.

Nutrient deficiency A lack of one of the nutrients essential for healthy plant growth. The symptoms of the nutrient deficiency are referred to as a disorder.

Obligate   Describes a parasite which is exclusively dependent upon living matter.

Parasitic fungi Fungi which feed on or in another living organism and give no benefit in return. They can cause disease and the death of plants. Parasitic fungi can be obligate or facultative.

Pathogen   Any organism causing a disease, be it fungus, bacterium or virus.

Physiological disorder A plant disorder due to environmental conditions, such as incorrect temperature, pH, or water levels, or extreme weather such as hail, strong wind, rain or drought.

Phytotoxic damage A plant disorder due to exposure to pollution or pesticides containing substances toxic to the plant. Symptoms may vary, but normally include discolouration, distortion and weakening of the plant.

Powdery mildew Whitish mycelium which coats leaves, stems and buds and is produced by a number of fungi species. It gives the affected parts a white powdery appearance, and these parts often become discoloured and distorted. It is a common fungal disease which slowly debilitates the host plant, which can suffer premature leaf-fall and eventual death. Powdery mildew is not related to downy mildew although the symptoms may appear the same.

Red thread A fungal disease which causes rot on lawns, especially on red fescue grass and on poor soils or after prolonged heavy rain. The grass dies out in roughly circular patches and appears red in colour with pink strands amongst the leaves.

Replant disease Poor growth of plants which have been newly-planted on land that has previously had the same or closely-related species grown on it. This is well known with roses and some fruit trees and the cause is thought to be a fungal pathogen that lives in the soil. The older plants were not greatly affected, but, when new ones are planted, their roots are very susceptible to the disease.

Reversion A serious disease of blackcurrants caused by a virus-like organism. This leads to severe reductions in cropping and changes in the appearance of the leaves. It is spread by the big-bug mite.

Rhizomorph Dense root-like strands produced by mycelium on certain fungi. They are dark in colour and look like bootlaces.

Rot The collapse of plant tissues due to a number of bacterial and fungal diseases. Root rot is the decay of the roots, soft rot is caused by bacterial diseases which attack fleshy roots and collar rot affects the base of the stem at soil level, usually following physical damage. Brown rot is a serious disease, chiefly of top fruit. It usually enters through damage on the skin of the fruit and rots the fruit either while it is still on the tree or after it has been harvested. It may also infect side shoots, causing die-back. Dry rot is a fungal disease which causes the dry decay and shrivelling of parts of plants, whilst wet rot causes soft and watery roots.

Russeting   Describes rough patches of cork occurring on the surface of top fruits caused by environmental conditions. Do not confuse with some apples and pears that are naturally russet-coloured.

TOP TIP

Preventing clematis wilt
Plant clematis sp. so that the root ball is 10cm below the soil surface to help prevent clematis wilt. Also, try to plant something in front of it to give the base shade or place rocks or slate at the base of the stem.

Rust   A fungal disease which produces small, powdery areas of fungal growth usually on the leaves. This growth is sometimes brown and rust-like but can be a range of colours. Different fungi species cause different types of rust, with variations in symptoms, on a wide range of garden plants. The fungi have complex lifecycles but basically they develop hyphae in the tissues of the host plant and drain the nutrients. Rust does not kill the plant but weakens it.

Scab   This is largely a fungal disease which mainly affects fruit, roots and tubers and is characterised by swollen, rough and corky lesions, although leaves may also be discoloured or blistered. The various fungi species which cause fruit scab overwinter either in the soil or on fallen leaves and then infect young leaves in the spring before being blown onto the surrounding fruit. Root scab persists in the soil as spores and infects the host via the root hairs before spreading.

Scorch   A disorder where the foliage dries out and turns brown either due to excessive sunlight, especially after watering in sunny weather, or fertiliser or pesticide applications which have wetted the leaves. Scorch can also affect the roots if an overdose of fertiliser or pesticide is given or if applications are made when the soil is too dry.

Smut   A disease caused by hundreds of fungi species which produce masses of black, soot-like spores. These spores can infect seed, the soil or the growing points of plants. The spores germinate and the mycelium then infects the rest of the plant. Smut may also be accompanied by distortion of the affected plant part and sometimes by spots on the leaves. Smut is unsightly and stunts the growth of the plant but rarely kills it outright. Smut spores can persist in the soil for several years.

Snow mould   A fungal disease which causes rot on lawns, especially on fine-leaved grasses and after cool damp periods. The grass rots and dies in roughly circular patches and appears yellow-brown in colour with grey or pink tints.

Sooty mould   A black, soot-like deposit which is the spores and mycelium of a fungus. It appears on the upper surfaces of leaves that are located beneath the feeding sites of sap-sucking insects. These insects secrete honeydew which coats the leaves and the fungus grows on these contaminated surfaces. The fungus that produces sooty mould does no direct damage to plants, but it does cut off sunlight to the leaves thus reducing photosynthesis. It may cause premature leaf-fall and weaken the plant.

Splitting   See *cracking.*

Spore   A minute structure of fungi consisting of one or two cells used for reproduction. Each fungus produces thousands of spores and these are spread by wind or water.

Spots   A plant disease caused by many species of fungi, bacteria and viruses on many different host plants. The disease is generally characterised by discolouration and distortion on areas of plant parts, mainly spots on the leaves. These spots range in colour depending upon the disease species but small black dots are almost certainly caused by fungi. The spots are generally small and regular in shape and destroy the plant tissue. The plant can form defence boundaries around these lesions to prevent the complete death of the plant part. Roses are susceptible to black spot, which is a fungal disease.

Toadstool   An example of a fruiting body of a fungus. It is born above ground on a stem with a parasol-like cap which contain the spores for reproduction. The toadstool can often be the only visible sign of the fungus by which identification is possible.

Viral disease A disease which is caused by a virus which lives in or on living plants.

Virus A sub-microscopic nucleoprotein structure which enters plant cells and takes over the organisation of the cell nucleus in order to reproduce. Most viruses are considered detrimental to plants, although some can infect a host plant and show no symptoms until the virus is transmitted through, for example, propagation.

Wilt A common and widespread fungal disease caused by a number of soil-born fungi. It attacks the vascular systems causing them to turn brown or black. Leaves wilt simultaneously, turn yellow and eventually shrivel. Die-back is rapid. It is thought that the fungus blocks the vascular systems or emits toxins which cause the plant to weaken and it may die. Wilt disease can persist in the soil for several years as mycelium or spores.

Witches' brooms Common on woody host plants especially birch, cherry and plum trees. From a distance they look like birds' nests but are in fact large clusters of closely growing, spurred twigs in the tree. They are caused by a number of agents, namely fungal, viral, pest and climatic, but they do little damage to the tree.

Control and prevention

Active ingredient The chemical ingredient within a pesticide which acts on the pest or pathogen to reduce the damage done to the plant. Most active ingredients do not kill the pest outright but focus on one part of the pest, for example, so that it cannot eat or develop into an adult.

Bacterial insecticide An insecticide which contains a parasitic bacterium which kills certain pest insects.

Bait Food which attracts animal pests, for example mice, and is laced with a chemical which causes the animal to die.

Biological control Using one organism to control another. This involves actively encouraging or deliberately introducing natural predators or parasites of a pest or disease on and around plants. Predatory insects, mites and nematodes and parasitic insects, fungi and bacteria are used to search out and kill pests and diseases. These organisms are most effective when released inside greenhouses or conservatories, for example, and they may either keep the problem at an acceptable level or completely remove it.

Calibrate An important process before applying pesticide via a knapsack sprayer. The area to be treated is measured, the application rate is calculated and the equipment is assessed so that the exact quantity of pesticide can be added to water for application.

Certified An official standard given to seeds, plants or stock, in this case to confirm that they are pest and disease-free.

Chemical control Using a selected chemical for reducing pests, diseases or weeds, ideally without harming humans, the affected plants, wildlife or the environment.

Collar A piece of material that is placed around the stem of the plant and lies on the soil surface. It helps prevent insects from laying their eggs in the soil surrounding the plant so that the emerging larvae hopefully do not chew through the stems.

Companion planting A method of cultural control which involves planting useful plants next to or near plants which are prone to attack by certain pests. A useful plant may be one with flowers which attracts insects such as hoverflies or lacewings which prey on aphids. Pungent-smelling plants may also be useful in deterring pests such as whitefly, and these can be planted in between the choice plants.

Compatible A pesticide which can be used in conjunction with other pesticides or controls with no harmful effects to the plant or biological control insects.

Contact pesticide An insecticide, fungicide and herbicide which only kills the pest, disease or weed with which it comes into contact.

Crop protection The prevention and control of undesirable pests, diseases and weeds to reduce the damage done to the desired plants. This will involve methods of biological control, chemical control and cultural control or a combination of these which is called integrated pest management.

Crop rotation A devised system of growing different groups of vegetables on a plot of land every year. The groups can be loosely divided according to family, such as legumes, Solanaceae, brassicas, Umbellifereae or onion, or based on what part of the plant is to be harvested such as seed, shoot, fruit, root, leaf or bulb. In reality only three or four groups are selected and rotated one after the other on the plot of land. A common system is to grow root vegetables, followed by legumes, followed by brassicas followed by bulbs. Crop rotation reduces soil-living pests and diseases which will reach epidemic proportions if allowed to thrive on one crop. It will also help keep soil nutrients balanced as one crop will deplete the soil of a particular nutrient over time.

Cultural control Preventing or reducing damaging organisms by a range of working methods. These include crop rotation, using disease-resistant cultivars, mechanical removal of pests, diseases and weeds, mulching, hygienic growing practices and companion planting.

Curative control Any reactive control method which reduces a pest or disease after it has entered a garden or greenhouse and damaged plants. This can include applying pesticides, trapping pest animals, pruning and burning diseased wood or weeding.

Drench Saturating the soil or growing media with a pesticide in a high volume of water. Biological controls such as nematodes are also applied as a drench.

Dust An insecticide which is formulated into a dust which coats plants to control a variety of pests.

Environmental condition Providing plants with the correct conditions in which to live and grow to ensure optimum health and natural resistance to pest and disease attack. This includes providing the correct temperature and sunlight levels, watering and feeding regimes and a balance of ventilation and humidity.

Environmental control Providing environmental conditions in which a pest or disease is discouraged from colonising or thriving. For example, thrips prefer hot and dry conditions so damping down an area or plant is an effective environmental control.

Fumigant A pesticide which is applied in the form of a smoke or gas to control vertebrate pests, insects or fungal diseases.

Fungicide A pesticide for fungal disease control.

Grease-banding A control method for trapping the wingless females of the winter moth. A band of sticky material is wrapped around the tree trunk about one metre above the ground so that when the females climb up the tree they become stuck to it and cannot reach the young shoots where they lay their eggs. Grease-banding is done before winter, and the material is removed and burnt in spring.

Growth regulator/growth retardant A chemical preparation which contains chemical hormones to alter or arrest the growth of animals, fungi or plants. It is used in certain pesticides to control pests, fungal diseases and weeds.

Harvest interval The period of time between spraying pesticides onto a crop and being able to safely harvest that crop.

Herbicide A chemical substance for weed control.

Hygiene Growing practices which ensure that materials, tools, plants and the environment in which the plants grow are clean. This means that pests, diseases and weeds are less likely to colonise plants or be spread from plant to plant. Good hygiene practices include using clean tools, sterilised soil and containers, clearing growing areas of weeds and plant debris, which can harbour pests and diseases, and removing and burning all diseased plants and wood.

TOP TIP

Preventing diseases from dust infecting plants
Lightly wet the floor of your greenhouse before sweeping up. It will make it easier and the dust which may carry diseases won't fly onto the plants.

Inorganic pesticide One which is not derived from living or dead organisms (plants and animals). Most modern pesticides are inorganic.

Insecticide A pesticide for insect control.

Integrated pest management Understanding and utilising all types of control measures available in order that they complement each other in the protection of plants against pests, diseases and weeds. Dependence on one method of pest control is undesirable and rarely effective therefore a combination of cultural control, biological control and chemical control is considered the most successful approach.

Jeyes Fluid A trade name for a common general horticultural detergent. It is a phenolic emulsion and can also be used as a partial soil steriliser.

Organic pesticide One which is derived from living or dead organisms (plants and animals) and therefore contains carbon. Most modern pesticides are inorganic. Some are derived from mineral sources and are deemed less environmentally destructive, but they are not truly organic.

Parasite   An organism which lives on or in another organism from which it obtains food but gives no benefit in return. Certain parasitic wasps, bacteria and fungi are used as biological controls for pests and diseases.

Personal protective equipment (PPE) Clothing and equipment required by law whilst preparing, using or disposing of pesticides. Items can include goggles, respirators, gloves, coveralls and boots and the pesticide label must contain the relevant information.

Pest control   Preventing or reducing the numbers of pests or diseases by cultural control, biological control or chemical control or a combination of these.

Pesticide   Any chemical substance formulated for the purpose of pest, disease or weed control. Various types of pesticide are classified according to the category of the problem, for example, insecticide for insect control, fungicide for fungal disease control or herbicide for weed control. Pesticides are available in a range of formulations including liquids, wettable powders, dusts, granules and smokes.

Pheromone trap A sticky card impregnated with male pheromones so that the female pest is attracted to it and gets stuck to it.

Plant protection compost Manufactured compost which contains certain pesticides, usually in a slow-release formulation, which help prevent pests and diseases which can occur especially in container-grown plants, for example, vine weevil or damping off.

Predator   An organism which seeks out and kills another organism for food. Certain predatory beetles, midges, mites and nematodes are used as biological controls for pests.

Pre-emergence The mode of action of certain herbicides which are applied to the soil and prevent weed seed from germinating. The herbicide forms a chemical layer in the top layer of the soil, above the roots of established plants, but to a sufficient depth to control weeds.

Preventative measure Any proactive control which prevents a pest, disease or weed from entering a garden or greenhouse and doing damage to plants. This can include constructing fences against large vertebrate pests, using

166

certified pest and disease-free stock, employing good hygiene practices, using a crop rotation system, or applying a mulch to beds and borders.

Residual   The mode of action of certain insecticides, fungicides and herbicides which are applied to the soil or foliage of plants and form a chemical layer or coating which remains after application. These pesticides kill pests, diseases and weeds which come into contact with the chemical at the time of application and for a certain period afterwards.

Residue   Any substance which remains after application on the surface of foliage, soil, paths or greenhouse structures.

Resistance   Describes a seed, plant or turf which has a natural defence or has been specially bred to resist pests, diseases or disorders.

Rogueing   Mechanically removing and destroying seeds, seedlings, plants or parts of plants which are dead, diseased or damaged, or are infested with a pest or are showing symptoms of a disorder. This is particularly applied to seedlings.

Scaring device   Any gadget which is located amongst plants in order to frighten away pest animals, particularly birds. Some gardeners hang CDs or tin foil amongst vegetables or newly-seeded lawns. These materials catch the sunlight which unnerves the bird so that it hopefully does not eat the seeds or plants. A scarecrow is a traditional device for deterring flocks of birds from crops.

Seed dressing   An outer coating which is applied to a seed and contains a chemical fungicide or insecticide. Seed dressings are usually only applied to seeds such as vegetables which are used for exhibition purposes.

Selective herbicide   Any herbicide which suppresses or kills certain weeds but does not affect other species. For example, it may kill dicotyledon weeds in lawns or kill monocotyledon weeds (usually grass) around dicotyledon ornamental plants.

Smoke   An insecticide or fungicide which is formulated to be lit and will smoulder and emit smoke. The active ingredient is released in the smoke and it is used as a fumigant to control pests and fungal diseases.

Soft soap   A soft soap which can be mixed with water and used as a spray to control soft-bodied insects such as aphids, mealybug or red spider mite. Savona is a trade name of a widely-used soft soap.

Soil-acting   The mode of action of certain herbicides and fungicides, which are applied to the soil and prevent weed seed and soil-borne fungal spores from germinating. The pesticide forms a chemical vapour in the top layer of the soil above the roots of established plants but to a sufficient depth to control weeds and fungal diseases.

Sterilisation   The removal of micro-organisms from the soil or growing media by steam or dry heat treatment. This kills pests, diseases and weed seeds. When sterilising soil, it is useful to note that soil bacteria are active from 3°C - 43°C, most are killed from 43°C - 71°C but some may survive at 100°C. Although saprophytic bacteria are beneficial in compost heaps, it is best to sterilise soil at above 71°C to ensure that most parasitic bacteria are killed. Equipment such as pots, knives and secateurs should be sterilised frequently especially if used in any propagation process. This is normally done with a bleach solution, Jeyes Fluid or similar. This should kill any pests and diseases.

Sticky trap   A piece of card with non-drying glue which is hung in glasshouses to trap flying insects. The card is a specific colour to attract specific insects, for example blue or yellow and is more of a pest indicator rather than a control method.

Symptom   The effects of a pest or disease organism on a plant. Symptoms are visible to the gardener either as changes to the plant organs, for example, discolouration of leaves, or to the plant itself, for example, wilt and death. The symptom, or symptoms, is important in identifying the pest or disease, in order that the appropriate control method can be chosen.

Systemic   The mode of action of certain insecticides, fungicides and herbicides which are applied to and absorbed by the foliage of a plant and then transported to other parts of the plant. This means that a systemic herbicide will kill the roots of a weed as well as the top growth and a systemic insecticide will kill the specific insect on most aerial parts of the plant. The term is used interchangeably with translocated.

Tar oil wash A tar-based liquid which is applied to deciduous trees and shrubs only in the winter months. It is especially used in December and early January to kill the eggs of aphids which overwinter on trunks and stems. This greatly reduces the initial infestation of those aphids in spring. The term is used interchangeably with winter wash.

Tolerance Describes a plant which can be infected by a disease or attacked by a pest but will survive and appear unharmed, especially if other pest control methods are employed. Fruit and vegetable cultivars are often chosen because of their specific pest or disease tolerance so that they will still produce a decent crop. The term can also describe the pest or disease which has an in-built tolerance to the pesticide used to control it. The pest or disease may be reduced but not removed altogether, or a stage in its lifecycle may remain present, for example the spores of a fungus or the adults of an insect, whilst the other stages are killed.

Total herbicide A herbicide which kills both dicotyledon and monocotyledon weeds. It is important to remember that if it is applied to desired plants they will be damaged as well and may die.

Translocated See *systemic*.

Tree guard Usually a thick plastic sheet which can be wrapped and secured around the base of a young tree to prevent damage to the bark by animal pests such as deer and rabbits.

Vector control Using a method of pest control to prevent or reduce a specific vector of a plant disease or disorder.

Weed control Preventing or reducing the numbers of weeds by cultural control, for example weeding or mulching, or chemical control, for example applying a herbicide, or a combination of these.

Weeding   The mechanical removal of weeds. Hand-weeding with a grubber, hand fork or border fork is best for removing perennial weeds or those which have set seed. Hoeing or rotavating are also options for controlling annual weeds which can be left to die on the surface of the soil in hot weather or incorporated into the soil.

Wetter/spreader A substance either present in or added to a pesticide to increase the coverage of the pesticide on the pest or foliage of a plant. It may also help the spray to penetrate closely-packed leaves or scales on a bud or bulb.

Winter wash See *tar oil wash*.

Tools, equipment and sundries

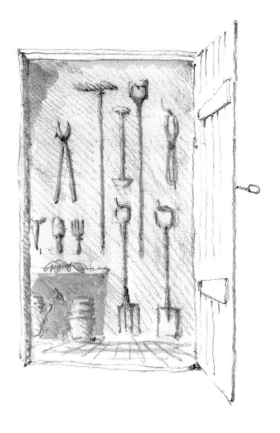

Tools and their parts

Adjustment screws Found on cylinder lawn mowers and used to adjust the height of the rollers and the proximity of the blades to the cutting plate.

Aerator Makes holes in turf by pushing tines into the surface. This helps to alleviate compaction and introduces air to the root zone.

Air filter Cleans the air which passes through an engine to cool it.

Besom broom A brush made with a bundle of twigs tied around a stick. It is used for sweeping or for spreading sand and topsoil into a lawn.

Billhook A hand-held tool which has a hooked blade with a sharp, straight outer edge. It is used for heavy pruning.

Blade A flat piece of metal with a sharp edge. On a lawn mower the blades spin round to cut the grass.

Bow saw A saw used to cut material of up to four inches.

Chainsaw A petrol-driven machine used to cut down trees and branches. The rotating chain is the cutting surface.

Chipper A machine that cuts wood into smaller pieces. Material such as branches and twigs are passed into the machine via a hopper and exit the machine as 'chips'.

Cultivator A hand-held tool used to break up soil. It usually has three angled prongs which are pushed into the soil then turned and lifted back out.

Cylinder mower A lawn mower which has blades mounted on a cylinder. This turns against a fixed metal plate to cut the grass. It usually has a roller mounted on the back and can be powered by petrol or electricity.

Distributor A tool to distribute seed and fertiliser onto soil or lawn and usually consists of a trough mounted on wheels. On a full width spreader, the material falls through holes in the bottom of the trough and onto the ground. On a spinning disc spreader the material firstly falls onto a plate which rotates and throws the material onto the surrounding ground. On both machines the holes can be manually opened and closed by a lever. The size of the holes is regulated according to the material and application rates.

Edging iron A tool with a long handle and a sharp metal end shaped like a half-moon. It is used for slicing turf to re-edge borders or make new areas in lawn. This term is used interchangeably with half moon.

Edging shears A scissor-like tool with long handles, used to cut the grass edges of lawn. The blades are set at right angles to the handles.

Fork A tool with prongs at the end which is used for weeding, turning the soil and prising plants out of the soil. A border fork is slightly smaller so can be used between plants more easily.

Gang mower A lawn mower which drags a number of cylinder blades behind it and has a seat for the operator.

Grass box Collects the grass clippings on a lawn mower. It is mounted at either the front or back of the mower.

Grass hook A tool like a short-handled scythe which is used for cutting grass and light brushwood.

Grecian saw Small hand-held saw which usually retracts into the handle and is used to cut material with a diameter up to two inches.

Grubber A small two-pronged implement used to prise out weeds and roots.

Half moon A tool with a long handle and a sharp metal end shaped like a half-moon. It is used for slicing turf to re-edge borders or make new areas in lawn. This term is used interchangeably with edging iron.

Hand fork A useful pronged tool for weeding and turning the soil over.

Hedge trimmer A petrol, battery or electric-powered tool with two moving blades which is used to cut or trim hedges.

Hoe A long-handled tool with a metal end used for weeding, loosening the surface of the soil or making drills in the soil. Different hoes have a variety of shaped ends according to their purpose. Some examples are draw hoe, drill hoe and swan neck hoe which are all pulled towards the user and a Dutch hoe which is pushed away from the

user. An onion hoe has a short handle and is used for weeding around plants.

Hollow tine   A prong with a hollow centre which takes out a core of soil.

Hopper   A container mounted onto a piece of machinery which holds and directs material, for example, seed into a distributor or twigs into a shredder.

Hover mower   Type of lawn mower which floats on a cushion of air and cuts grass with a slashing motion. It can be powered by petrol or electricity.

Knapsack sprayer   A piece of equipment used for applying pesticides to an area of ground or plants. The diluted pesticide solution is contained in the plastic knapsack and is directed onto the ground or plants by the operator via a pressurised lance.

Leaf blower   Petrol or electric-powered tool which blows out air and is used for pushing debris, usually fallen leaves, into one area to make them easier to collect.

Loot   A long-handled tool with a reversible metal plate at the bottom. The rough side of the plate is for spreading topsoil and sand around a lawn and the smoother side is used for rubbing the material into the lawn.

Lopers   A long-handled tool for cutting twigs and branches with a diameter between half and three quarters of an inch.

Nipples   Metal protrusions with small holes found on machinery with moving parts. Grease which lubricates the moving parts is applied via the nipples using a grease gun.

Pen-knife   A small bladed knife which folds back into its handle. 'Swiss Army' knives are examples where a variety of blades and tools are held within one handle. Very useful.

Pitch fork   This is much like a fork but the prongs are thinner and slightly curved and the tool tends to be lighter. It is very useful for moving large quantities of bulky material such as compost or straw.

Power hose/power washer An electric-powered tool which pumps water at high pressures through a hand-regulated nozzle. It is used for cleaning surfaces such as moss-covered paths and glass in greenhouses.

Propagation knife A small hand-held knife with a sharp blade used for cutting soft stems and leaves. It is very much like a pen-knife which is often used instead.

Pruning knife A small hand-held knife with a sharp and slightly curved blade used for stripping branches and twigs. It is very much like a pen-knife which is often used instead.

Pruning saw   Small hand-held saw which usually retracts into the handle and is used to cut material with a diameter of up to two inches.

Pull cord   String with a handle which is pulled to start a machine's engine.

Rake   A long-handled tool with prongs at the end, set at right angles to the handle which is drawn across the surface which is being raked. Metal rakes are used to break the soil down into a fine tilth by working it back and forward across the soil surface. Landscape rakes have wooden prongs and are used to break up large clods of soil and generally level the soil surface. Plastic and hard rubber rakes are used for moving general debris like leaves and twigs. Springbok rakes have flexible metal prongs and are generally used to scarify turf.

Roller   A heavy metal cylinder at the back of a lawn mower which produces a striped effect on lawns.

Rotary mower A lawn mower which cuts grass with a slashing motion as the blades sweep over the grass. It can be petrol or electric-powered and can have a roller mounted on the back.

Rotavator	A rotary cultivator which has a series of adjustable blades for cutting through soil and turning it over to variable depths. It can be pushed or powered by petrol.
Scalpel	Razor blade mounted in a handle and used for cutting soft stems and leaves in propagation.
Scarifier	A machine with metal prongs for raking the surface of turf in order to remove the build up of grass thatch. A springbok rake can also be used as a scarifier.
Scythe	A long-handled 'traditional' tool for cutting grass and harvesting cereals, etc. The blade is narrow and slightly curved.
Secateurs	Hand-held tool used for pruning twigs to a diameter of half an inch. Bybass secateurs use two blades in a scissor action and anvil secateurs use one blade cutting onto a flat plate.
Shears	Large hand-held scissor-like tool used to cut soft material such as long grass and hedges.
Shovel	A spade-like tool but with a larger blade which has a curved edge and is used for moving material such as soil, sand and gravel.
Shredder	A machine which shreds dry vegetative material. Material such as leaves, stems and twigs are passed into the machine via a hopper and exit as smaller pieces, ideal for putting on the compost heap.
Sickle	A short-handled tool used for cutting or harvesting. The blade is narrow and curved in a semi-circular shape.
Slit tine	A flattened metal spike which is a part on an aerator.
Solid tine	A cylindrical metal spike which is a part on an aerator.
Spade	A tool with a sharp blade generally used for digging soil.
Spark plug	This part causes an engine to start and then run continuously by producing a spark which ignites the petrol.
Spiker	A machine used to make holes in turf. This helps to alleviate compaction and introduces air to the root zone.
Spit	The metal blade on a spade. The term also describes the depth of soil to be removed whilst digging.

Sprung tines The prongs on a springbok rake which are flexible.

Strimmer A hand-held power tool with a rotating plastic cord at its end, which cuts through material such as grass which is too long for a lawn mower to handle or which grows on uneven ground.

Tine Another word for a prong or spike and can be found on a fork, rake and aerator.

Tiner A hand-held tool traditionally used to make holes in turf. The tines are placed onto the soil and then pushed in using the foot. It is designed so that the tines rise back out of the soil when the foot pressure is released. This helps to alleviate soil compaction and introduces air to the root zone.

Trowel A hand-held tool like an elongated spoon used to dig small holes in soil, usually for planting.

Turf cutter A powered tool which cuts and lifts sections of turf.

Turfing iron A spade-like tool with a triangular blade which is angled upwards from the handle and is used by slicing under, and then lifting, the turf.

2-stroke Refers to the number of strokes an engine takes to produce power. The term is more commonly used to describe the type of fuel mix for a piece of machinery. (In horticultural machines the fuel mix is usually 50:1 or 25:1 petrol to oil.)

4-stroke Refers to the number of strokes an engine takes to produce power. The term is more commonly used to describe the type of fuel for a piece of machinery. (Unleaded petrol is also used in 4-stroke engines.)

Equipment and sundries

Batter board A wooden board used as a guide for cutting hedges to the required gradient.

Canes Bamboo stems cut into varying lengths and used to support plants.

Capillary matting Felt-like material used in greenhouses under pots of plants. If the plant is watered from the top of the pot, any surplus water that drains out of the bottom is absorbed by the matting which then allows the plants to take up this water when needed. Alternatively the matting is used as the watering system and the plants take up water from the bottom of the pot.

Cloche A mobile protective structure, traditionally a glass bell, which is placed over a plant. It is used mainly to raise early crops or to give frost protection to tender perennials. It can also be used to keep plants dry in the winter. Glass is still the preferred material, although clear polythene is often used.

Dibber A pencil-like implement which is used to make holes in soil for planting seedlings or to ease seedlings out of pots. Larger dibbers can be used to make holes in which to sow seeds or plant bulbs outdoors.

Diluter A canister, normally metal, which delivers liquid fertiliser at a measured rate. Concentrated fertiliser is mixed with water, put into the diluter and then topped up with water. The inlet on the diluter is then attached to a water supply and the outlet attached to a hose to spray onto the plants or soil.

Ear defenders An item of safety equipment, like huge headphones, which blocks out a large amount of the noise from machinery.

Fleece A lightweight thin material which allows water and light to pass through. It is used as frost and wind protection for young and tender plants, and to create a microclimate around plants such as young vegetables to give them an early start.

Galvanised wire Flexible iron wire coated with zinc to protect it from rust.

Goggles An item of safety equipment, these are plastic glasses worn to prevent injury to the eyes.

Grease gun A tool which pumps grease out of a nozzle and is used for lubricating parts of machinery.

Hand sprayer A hand-held plastic canister with a nozzle and a trigger-like handle for applying a fine mist of water, pesticides or fertiliser to the foliage of a plant.

Hanging basket A container used for plants which have long lax growth and will therefore trail down from the basket. They are generally made of plastic, wire or wood and can be planted straight into or have pots placed inside them.

Hessian A sacking material used 'traditionally' as frost and wind protection for plants. Modern alternatives are fleece and polythene.

Hose Flexible plastic pipe for watering.

Irrigation A general term referring to a system which waters.

Lance A hollow rod usually attached to a hose to regulate hand-watering by a lever and handle.

Lawn edging Plastic, metal and wood materials used to contain and separate lawn edges from borders, beds and paths.

Long tom A pot which is twice as long as its diameter. It is used for plants with deeper root systems or bulbs.

Mallet An entirely wooden hammer with an enlarged cubed head. It is used to hammer brittle items such as bamboo canes into soil.

Mesh A hard but flexible plastic material with perforations used for fencing, supporting plants, placing in gutters to catch leaves and for laying on grass paths to reduce wear.

Mister A plastic canister with a nozzle and a trigger-like handle for applying a fine mist of water to the foliage of plants.

179

Modular tray   A plastic tray for germinating seed which is rectangular and shallow and divided into square compartments. Individual seed, or groups of seed, can be sown in each compartment so that there is less root disturbance when pricking out.

Netting   A soft and flexible plastic material with perforations used to protect ponds and vegetables from birds and debris. It is also used as a plant support or for shading.

Pan   A pot or tray which is wider than it is deep and is used for sowing seeds or growing plants with shallow root systems such as most alpine and succulent plants.

Pea sticks   Lengths of stems and twigs usually cut from coppiced hazel in early spring. The twigs are pushed into the ground next to plants which require support, hence the name 'pea' sticks as peas have traditionally been supported in this way. Hazel is used because the twigs are flexible so can be woven together to form cages over and around the plant. It is best to use them soon after cutting because if they are too dry they do not bend and can break.

Polythene   A type of clear plastic which can be used to clad greenhouses instead of glass. It is also used to protect individual plants from frost and rain.

Pot   A container in which plants are grown. They are commonly made of plastic or clay but also of fibre-glass or stone. They have holes in the base for drainage and come in varying sizes measured by either the diameter or the capacity.

Propagator   A mini-greenhouse comprising of at least a tray base and clear lid into which pots of seeds or cuttings are placed. It creates a warm and humid micro-climate within a greenhouse or on the windowsill. Some propagators come with small ventilation holes and electric heating systems at their base.

Raffia   A fibre from the raffia palm which is traditionally used for string or to hold grafting and budding joins together.

Rooting hormone   A synthetic hormone in powdered or liquid form into which the base cuts of cuttings are dipped to aid the formation of roots.

Rose	An attachment fitted to the spout of a watering can or lance which has holes in the end to produce a fine spray.
Seed tray	A plastic container used for germinating seed. It is a rectangular shape, about A4 paper size, has a shallow depth and has drainage holes in the base. A half tray is similar but half the size.
Seep hose	A hose which has minute holes along its length and is used as part of an irrigation system. The hose is placed on or just under the soil and can be left unattended to provide the area with water.
Sieve	A wire mesh with metal or wooden sides which is shaken by hand to separate material into coarse and fine parts. For example, stones from soil or seeds from seed heads can be separated.
Sprinkler	A device used to automatically distribute water. It is connected to a hose and produces a fine spray in an oscillating or rotating manner.
Stake	A pole used to support plants by driving it into the soil and securing the plant to it. It can be made of wood, bamboo cane, metal or plastic.
Steel toecap boots	Safety boots with steel under the leather in the toe area to protect the feet.
Swell gel	Silica granules which absorb moisture, swell up and then release the moisture gradually. The granules are placed in the bottom of planting holes to provide more water around the roots of plants. Swell gel is especially used in areas with dry springs or summers or on free-draining soils which dry out quickly.
Tamper	An implement for firming soil especially in pots and trays. It is usually home-made, fashioned out of wood with a small handle, and fits loosely into a pot about 1cm down from the rim.
Thermometer	A gauge for measuring temperature. It is usually glass and contains a cylinder of mercury which expands and contracts with fluctuations in air temperature.
Tree guard	A plastic sleeve which is placed around the trunk of a young tree or sapling to protect the bark from animals such as deer.

Tree tie   A soft plastic belt which is used to tie a trunk, stem or branch to a stake or wire. It has a movable buffer which can be situated between the plant and support to reduce wind-rock and damage to the plant.

Trellis   Plastic, metal or wooden strips attached in a criss-cross fashion to provide a supporting structure for climbing plants.

Trug   A shallow wooden basket 'traditionally' used for collecting cut flowers, vegetables and fruit from the garden.

Twine   Garden string, usually made from a strong fibre. It is often treated with a tar so that the twine does not weather so readily.

Vine eye   A large nail which is driven or screwed into the mortar course of a wall. The head end has a circle with a hole for holding wire.

Wall nail   A large nail which is driven into the mortar course of a wall. The head end is soft metal for bending over and securing branches and stems.

Watering can   A container for water with a long thin spout to which a rose can be attached. Used for watering plants!

WD40   Trade name for a lubricant which drives out water from metal and is used to keep tools from rusting. Usually sold in liquid spray form.

Weed control fabric   A meshed fabric which allows water but not light to penetrate. It is placed on the surface of the ground to help eradicate weeds. It is useful in the vegetable garden where young plants are planted through the fabric, or to clean weedy ground over a long period.

Wheelbarrow   A small cart for moving garden debris and materials. It consists of a metal frame with handles with one wheel at the front and two metal rests at the rear. Lifting the handles allows the wheelbarrow to be pushed along. Traditionally wheelbarrows were made of wood, but now metal or rigid plastic is used.

Appendices

Appendices

Weights and measures and conversions

Metric linear measurements

mm	=	millimetre	10 mm	=	1cm	1 mm = 0.039 in
cm	=	centimetre	100 cm	=	1m	1 cm = 0.394 in
m	=	metre	1000 m	=	1km	1 m = 1.094 yd
km	=	kilometre				1 km = 0.6214 mile

Imperial linear measurements

in	=	inch	1 in	=	1 ft	1 in = 25.4 mm
ft	=	foot	3 ft	=	1 yd	1 ft = 0.3048 m
yd	=	yard	1760 yd	=	1 mile	1 yd = 0.9144 m
						1 mile = 1.609 km

Metric capacity measurements

ml	=	millilitre	10 ml	=	1 cl	1 ml = 0.002 pt
cl	=	centilitre	1000 ml	=	1 l	1 cl = 0.018 pt
l	=	litre	100 cl	=	1 l	1 l = 1.76 pt
						10 l = 2.2 gal

Imperial capacity measurements

fl oz	=	fluid ounce	20 fl oz	=	1 pt	1 fl oz = 0.0296 l
pt	=	pint	8 pt	=	1 gal	1 pt = 0.568 l
gal	=	gallon				1 gal = 4.546 l

Metric weight measurements

mg	=	milligram	1000 mg	=	1 g	1 g = 0.03527 oz
g	=	gram	1000 g	=	1 kg	1 kg = 2.205 lb
kg	=	kilogram	1000 kg	=	1 tonne	1 tonne = 0.984 ton

Imperial weight measurements

oz	=	ounce	16 oz	=	1 lb	1 oz = 8.35 g
lb	=	pound	14 lb	=	1 stone	1 lb = 0.4536 kg
cwt	=	hundredweight	112 lb	=	1 cwt	1 stone = 6.35 kg
			160 stone/20 cwt	=	1 ton	1 ton = 1.016 tonne

Area measurements

1 hectare	=	10,000 square metres
1 acre	=	4,840 square yards
1 hectare	=	2.471 acres
1 acre	=	0.405 hectares
1 square mile	=	640 acres
1 square mile	=	259 hectares
1 square kilometre	=	100 hectares
1 square kilometre	=	247acres

Seasons (UK)

January	February	March	April
Mid Winter	Late Winter	Early Spring	Mid Spring

May	June	July	August
Late Spring	Early Summer	Mid Summer	Late Summer

September	October	November	December
Early Autumn	Mid Autumn	Late Autumn	Early Winter

This seasonal year is a guide based on the middle of the country. Winter may last longer in the north and Spring may start earlier in the south.

Beaufort scale of wind speed

Beaufort number	Kilometers per hour	Description of conditions
0	<1	calm smoke rises vertically
1	1-6	light air smoke drifts
2	7-12	light breeze wind felt on face, leaves rustle, vanes moved by wind
3	13-19	gentle breeze leaves and small twigs in constant motion, light flags extended
4	20-30	moderate breeze dust and loose paper raised, small branches move
5	31-39	fresh breeze small trees sway
6	40-50	strong breeze large branches move, telegraph wires whistle
7	51-62	near gale whole trees in motion, inconvenience felt in walking against the wind
8	63-74	gale twigs broken off trees, walking upright difficult
9	75-87	strong gale chimney pots and slates removed
10	88-102	storm trees uprooted, considerable structural damage
11	103-117	violent storm very rare on land, causing widespread damage
12	118+	hurricane

Temperature

°F	°C		°C	°F	
-40	-40		-40	-40	
-10	-23		-10	14	
0	-18		0	32	
10	-12		10	50	
20	-7		20	68	
30	-1		30	86	
40	4		40	104	
50	10		50	122	
60	16		60	140	
70	21		70	158	
80	27		80	176	
90	32		90	194	
100	38		100	212	

F = Fahrenheit
C= Celsius or Centigrade
° = degrees

Water boils at 100°C and 212°F
Water freezes at 0°C and 32°F

To convert from Celsius to Fahrenheit: multiply by 9, divide by 5 and add 32.

To convert from Fahrenheit to Celsius: subtract 32, multiply by 5 and divide by 9.

pH scale

0	1	2	3	4	5	6	7	8	9	10	11	12	13	14

acid   neutral   alkaline

This scale is logarithmic so, for example, pH1 is ten times more acid than pH2.

Soil particle sizes

>2 mm	gravel	o
0.2 mm - 2 mm	coarse sand	o
0.02 mm - 0.2 mm	fine sand	.
0.002 mm - 0.02 mm	silt	.
<0.002 mm	clay	.

Soil types (UK)

sand → loamy sand → sandy loam → sandy silt loam → silt loam → sandy clay loam → clay loam → silty clay loam → sandy clay → silty clay → clay.

Biological classification

Kingdom (Subkingdom)

Division (Subdivision, Superclass)

Class (Subclass, Infraclass)

Order (Suborder, Superfamily)

Family (Subfamily, Tribe)

Genus (**Species**, Subspecies)

All species fall into the category in bold type. The other categories may be omitted in smaller or less complex species.

Inflorescences

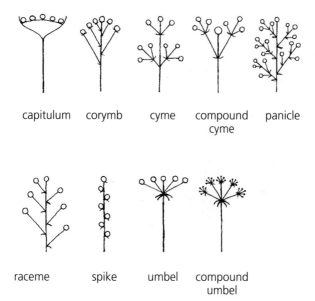

capitulum   corymb   cyme   compound cyme   panicle

raceme   spike   umbel   compound umbel

Leaf shapes

Simple

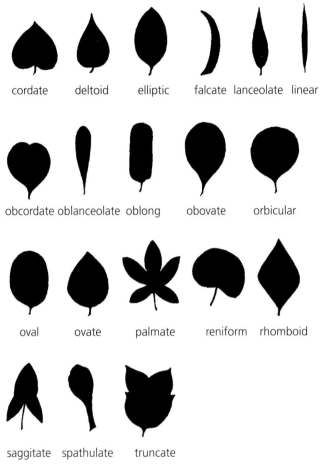

cordate   deltoid   elliptic   falcate   lanceolate   linear

obcordate   oblanceolate   oblong   obovate   orbicular

oval   ovate   palmate   reniform   rhomboid

saggitate   spathulate   truncate

Compound

pinnate   bipinnate   tripinnate   trifoliate   digitate   biternate

Index

Further reading

A History of British Gardening, Miles Hadfield, Penguin

Expert series, Dr D G Hessayon, Expert Books

John Brookes' Garden Design Book, John Brookes, Dorling Kindersley

Pests, Diseases & Disorders of Garden Plants, Buczacki & Harris, Collins

Plant Names Simplified, A T Johnson & H A Smith, Landsmans Bookshop Ltd

Plant Propagation, Principles & Practices, Hudson Thomas Hartmann (Editor), et al, Prentice Hall

Principles of Horticulture, C R Adams, K M Bamford, M P Early, Butterworth-Heinemann

RHS Encyclopedia of Garden Plants, Editor-in-Chief Christopher Brickell, Dorling Kindersley

RHS Encyclopedia of Gardening, Editor-in-Chief Christopher Brickell, Dorling Kindersley

RHS Gardeners Yearbook, Dorling Kindersley

Right Plant Right Place, Nicola Ferguson, Summit Books

The Complete Book of Plant Propagation, various contributors, Mitchell Beazley

The Nature & Property of Soils, N C Brady & R R Weil, Prentice Hall

The Organic Garden Book, Geoff Hamilton, Dorling Kinderlsey

The Pruner's Handbook, John Malins, David & Charles

What Perennial Where, Roy Lancaster, Dorling Kindersley